APPLIED DEVELOPMENTAL SCIENCE
Volume 10, Number 2 **2006**

SPECIAL ISSUE;
THE MULTIPLE CONTEXTS OF YOUTH DEVELOPMENT

ARTICLES

Applied Developmental Science
2006, Vol. 10, No. 2, 58–60

The Multiple Contexts of Youth Development: Implications for Theory, Research, and Practice

Lise M. Youngblade
University of Florida

Christina Theokas
Tufts University

Our goal for this special issue of *Applied Developmental Science* was to bring together articles addressing several key themes related to optimizing adolescent development through reducing risky behavior and promoting positive youth development. These themes include a focus on multiple contexts of development, the use of multidisciplinary approaches and mixed methods for understanding adolescent behavior, the inclusion of both positive and negative developmental outcomes, and attention to applied and policy implications. In other words, these articles embody a broad focus on applied developmental science (Lerner, 2004; Lerner, Fisher, & Weinberg, 2000).

Adolescence is a time of increased risky behavior. Although some risk-taking may be a positive force in development (Baumrind, 1987; Fischhoff, 1992; Shedler & Block, 1990), risky activities such as illegal drug use and unprotected sexual intercourse can be dangerous. Risky behaviors may occur individually but are often interrelated, are often established during youth, and often extend into adulthood (Jessor, 1998). These largely preventable behaviors can lead to negative outcomes that disrupt lives and have enormous costs to society (Gans, Alexander, Chu, & Elster, 1995; Kann et al., 1996; Zimmer-Gembeck, Alexander, & Nystrom, 1997; Ziv, Boulet, & Slap, 1999). In fact, public health researchers estimate that the annual cost to the United States that is due to morbidities related to adolescent risky behavior is more than $33 billion (Gans et al., 1995).

More recently, however, researchers and policy makers have begun to embrace the notion that optimal youth development owes not simply to a reduction in negative behavior but the growth of strengths and competencies that will prepare youth for the future. Healthy development embodies happiness and a sense of purpose and meaningful relationships that leads to youth being engaged and contributing to their families, schools, communities, and society. Accordingly, growing attention is focused on promoting positive youth development, encouraging health-promoting behavior, and investing in resources for youth (Benson, Leffert, Scales, & Blyth, 1998; Hawkins, Catalano, & Miller, 1992; Lerner & Simi, 2000). In other words, a focus on positive youth development is an active promotion of adolescents' competence, confidence, character, caring, and connection (see, e.g., Lerner et al., 2005) through aligning these capacities with resources in the ecology. Thus, a holistic approach to optimizing adolescent development requires an understanding of factors related to both reducing negative risk-taking behavior and increasing positive, competent youth behavior.

In the past two decades, significant effort has gone into developing comprehensive models of the role of multiple contextual domains (i.e., relations among individual characteristics, social relationships, and larger effects of communities and institutions) on adolescent behavior, and that include both risk and protective factors (Becker, Rankin, & Rickel, 1998; Hawkins et al., 1992; Jessor, 1998; Taylor & Wang, 2000). For example, Jessor proposed a model that includes five interrelated domains of risk and protective factors (biology and genetics, social environment, perceived environment, personality, behavior) that lead to adolescent risk behavior and lifestyles, and ultimately to health- and life-compromising outcomes. More broadly, working from the perspective of developmental systems theory and contextual psychology, researchers theorize that behaviors arise from the dynamic, bidirectional interaction between a person and multiple levels of his or her ecology (e.g., Bronfenbrenner & Morris, 2006; Lerner, 2006; Magnusson & Stattin, 2006; Petraitis, Flay, & Miller, 1995). Youth will thrive when there is a goodness of fit between individual developmental needs and contextual resources (Chess & Thomas, 1999; Lerner, Dowling, & Anderson, 2003). In addition, researchers in the field of developmental psychopathology suggest that multiple contextual factors influence both competent and risky developmental trajectories (e.g., Cicchetti & Aber, 1998; Cummings, Davies, & Campbell, 2000; Masten & Curtis, 2000; Sroufe, 1997). Thus, there is a compelling theoretical

Correspondence should be sent to Lise M. Youngblade, Ph.D., Institute for Child Health Policy, University of Florida, 1329 SW 16th Street, Room 5130, Gainesville, FL 32608. E-mail: lmy@ichp.ufl.edu

basis from which to consider behavior and development as a function of individuals' interactions with multiple developmental contexts.

Empirical research is congruent with this proposition. In fact, multiple contexts have been studied in previous research in terms of their connections to various adolescent behaviors, although more often than not, the focus is on single contexts. Predominantly, studies have included the worlds of the family, peers, and school, with much less attention, until recently, toward larger contexts, such as neighborhoods and communities (Brooks-Gunn, Duncan, & Aber, 1997; Leventhal & Brooks-Gunn, 2000). The articles herein all address multiple contexts and expand an analysis of context beyond what is typically examined. Although the number of contexts and characteristics examined varies across the articles, all focus attention on more than one context. In addition, the contexts included are those both proximal to the individual (e.g., family, peers) as well as those that are more distal (media influence, health care, communities, and neighborhoods). Together, these articles provide a rich, detailed portrait of family, friend, and media influences on adolescents' competent and delinquent behavior (Graber, Nichols, Lynne, Brooks-Gunn, & Botvin, this issue); the worlds of families, schools, and neighborhoods and their contributions to positive youth development (Theokas & Lerner, this issue); sibling caretaking and school outcomes (East, Weisner, & Reyes, this issue); and influences of families, peers, schools, and communities on adolescent risky and health-promoting behavior (Youngblade & Curry, this issue).

Beyond a focus on multiple contexts, the authors of the articles in this issue also bring to bear multiple theoretical approaches and diverse methods to their analyses. Athough all of the articles in this issue are congruent with basic propositions of developmental systems theory, the authors broaden this theoretical foundation by including, for example, relevance for prevention science (Graber et al., this issue), a sociological focus on kinship and family systems theories (East et al., this issue), insights from demography (Theokas & Lerner, this issue), and public health (Youngblade & Curry, this issue). These studies also creatively utilize multiple and varied methods including longitudinal approaches, the inclusion of reports from multiple parties, and objective data from the Census and state health insurance programs.

As stated previously, a holistic approach to adolescent health and well-being includes a focus on both the reduction of negative behavior and the promotion of positive and competent behavior, and all of the articles in this issue address both dimensions. That being said, there are multiple and varied ways of doing so—with different implications for theory and application. For example, one can focus on single indicators (e.g., tobacco use or exercise) or global composites of behavior (e.g., risky behavior or health-promoting behavior composites). Indeed, the articles in this issue vary in terms of the level of specificity or generality in the outcomes. For example, in predicting positive behavioral outcomes, both the articles by Theokas and Lerner (this issue) and that by Youngblade and Curry (this issue) utilize global indexes of positive behavior, whereas the articles by East et al. (this issue) and Graber et al. (this issue) identify specific indicators of competence. Similar variation is evident in terms of negative behavior as well. The point to be made, however, is that both approaches are of value. For example, although evidence has shown that risky behaviors are often interrelated (e.g., Dryfoos, 1990; Perkins & Borden, 2003), an alternative view of risk engagement targets such behaviors individually (Guilamo-Ramos, Litardo, & Jaccard, 2005). In their review of studies of adolescent risk behaviors, Guilamo-Ramos et al. reported that the mean correlation between risk behaviors was roughly 0.35, demonstrating that much of the variance in behavior was attributed to unique rather than common causes. Thus, studies that examine the dynamics of individual behaviors may provide valuable information for prevention program development. On the other hand, programs targeting adolescent risk behavior in generally healthy populations may benefit from a more generalist approach that recognizes the interrelation of specific types of risk behavior. The same can be said for conceptualizations of positive and competent behavior. Nevertheless, given that all the articles include both positive and negative developmental outcomes, it is possible to assess if they are predicted by similar or different contextual conditions that can inform the development of programs and policy.

Finally, in keeping with the mission and intent of the field of applied developmental science, the articles in this issue all speak to direct targets for intervention, prevention, and policy. For example, Graber et al. (this issue) highlight issues related to youth's engagement with violent media and the importance of parental monitoring. Youngblade and Curry (this issue) similarly describe monitoring and control at the parent and community level and draw policy-related connections to the health care system. Theokas and Lerner (this issue) underscore the importance of resource investments in the ecology of youth development. East and her colleagues (this issue) emphasize teachable points relevant to pregnancy prevention programs. In point of fact, the truly exciting aspect of all of these articles is that they suggest concrete intervention and policy objectives that are doable. As such, they point toward specific and quantifiable actions that can be, and should be, a fundamental part of any serious, multilevel, multicontext commitment to optimizing youth development.

As should be evident by now, as the coeditors of this issue of *Applied Developmental Science*, we are truly excited by this special issue. As a set, and individually, these articles build on the growing literature addressing optimal youth development. The articles illuminate the effects of risk and protective factors at multiple levels of contextual influence. The authors approach the topic from a multidisciplinary framework and utilize multiple and varied methods for understanding adolescent behavior. In contrast to much previous work, both positive and negative dimensions of behavioral outcomes are included. Finally, applied and policy relevant connections are explicated. As we stated at the outset, our goal was to compile a group of articles that embody a broad focus on applied developmental science as it relates to youth development. We believe we have exceeded that goal, and invite you to read the articles and accompanying commentary by John Schulenberg (this issue).

References

Baumrind, D. (1987). A developmental perspective on adolescent risk taking in contemporary America. *New Directions for Child Development, 37,* 93–125.

Becker, E., Rankin, E., & Rickel, A. U. (1998). *High-risk sexual behavior.* New York: Plenum.

Benson, P. L., Leffert, N., Scales, P. C., & Blyth, D. A. (1998). Beyond the "village" rhetoric: Creating healthy communities for children and adolescents. *Applied Developmental Science, 2,* 138–159.

Bronfenbrenner, U., & Morris, P. A. (2006). The bioecological model of human development. In R. M. Lerner (Ed.), *Theoretical models of human development. Handbook of Child Psychology* (Vol. 1, 6th ed., pp. 793–828). Hoboken, NJ: Wiley.

Brooks-Gunn, J., Duncan, G. J., & Aber, J. L. (Eds.). (1997). *Neighborhood poverty: Context and consequences for children* (Vol. I). New York: Russell Sage Foundation.

Chess, S., & Thomas, A.(1999). *Goodness-of-fit: Clinical applications from infancy through adult life.* Philadelphia: Bruner/Mazel.

Cicchetti, D., & Aber, J. L. (1998). Contextualism and developmental psychopathology. *Development and Psychopathology, 10,* 137–141.

Cummings, E. M., Davies, P. T., & Campbell, S. B. (2000). *Developmental psychopathology and family process.* New York: Guilford.

Dryfoos, J. G. (1990). *Adolescents at risk: Prevalence and prevention.* New York: Oxford University Press.

Fischhoff, B. (1992). Risk taking: A developmental perspective. In J. F. Yates (Ed.), *Risk-taking behavior* (pp. 133–162). New York: Wiley.

Gans, J. E., Alexander, B., Chu, R. C., & Elster, A. B. (1995). The cost of comprehensive preventive medical services for adolescents. *Archives of Pediatric and Adolescent Medicine, 149,* 1226–1234.

Guilamo-Ramos, V., Litardo, H. A., & Jaccard, J. (2005). Prevention programs for reducing adolescent problem behaviors: Implications of the co-occurrence of problem behaviors in adolescence, *Journal of Adolescent Health, 36,* 82–86.

Hawkins, J. D., Catalano, R. F., & Miller, J. Y. (1992). Risk and protective factors for alcohol and other drug problems in adolescence and early adulthood: Implications for substance abuse prevention. *Psychological Review, 112,* 64–105.

Jessor, R. (Ed.) (1998). *New perspectives on adolescent risk behavior.* Cambridge, England: Cambridge University Press.

Kann, L., Warren, C. W., Harris, W. A., Collins, J. L., Williams, B. I., Ross, J. G., et al. (1996). Youth risky behavior surveillance—United States, 1995. *Journal of School Health, 66,* 365–377.

Lerner, R. M. (2004). *Liberty: Thriving and civic engagement among America's youth.* Thousand Oaks, CA: Sage.

Lerner, R. M. (2006). Developmental science, developmental systems, and contemporary theories of human development. In R. M. Lerner (Ed.), *Theoretical models of human development. Handbook of Child Psychology* (Vol. 1, 6th ed., pp. 1–17). Hoboken, NJ: Wiley.

Lerner, R. M., Dowling, E. M., & Anderson, P. M. (2003). Positive youth development: Thriving as the basis of personhood and civil society. *Applied Developmental Science, 7,* 172–180.

Lerner, R. M., Fisher, C. B., & Weinberg, R. A. (2000). Toward a science for and of the people: Promoting civil society through the application of developmental science. *Child Development, 71*(1), 11–20.

Lerner, R. M., Lerner, J. V., Almerigi, J., Theokas, C., Phelps, E., Gestsdottir, S., et al. (2005). Positive youth development, participation in community youth development programs, and community contributions of fifth grade adolescents: Findings from the first wave of the 4-H Study of Positive Youth Development. *Journal of Early Adolescence, 25,* 17–71.

Lerner, R. M., & Simi, N. L. (2000). A holistic, integrated model of risk and protection in adolescence: A developmental contextual perspective about research, programs, and policies. In L. Bergman & R. Cairns (Eds.), *Developmental science and the holistic approach* (pp. 421–443). Mahwah, NJ: Lawrence Erlbaum Associates, Inc.

Leventhal, T., & Brooks-Gunn, J. (2000). The neighborhoods they live in: The effects of neighborhood residence on child and adolescent outcomes. *Psychological Bulletin, 126, 309–337.*

Magnusson, D., & Stattin, H. (2006). The person in the environment: Towards a General Model for Scientific Inquiry. In R. M. Lerner (Ed.), *Theoretical models of human development. Handbook of Child Psychology* (Vol. 1, 6th ed., pp. 400–464). Hoboken, NJ: Wiley.

Masten, A. S., & Curtis, W. J. (2000). Integrating competence and psychopathology: Pathways toward a comprehensive science of adaptation in development. *Development and Psychopathology, 12,* 529–550.

Perkins, D. F., & Borden, L. M. (2003). Positive behaviors, problem behaviors, and resiliency in adolescents. In R. M. Lerner, M. A. Easterbrooks, & J. Mistry (Eds.), *Handbook of psychology: Vol. 6. Developmental psychology* (pp. 373–394). New York: Wiley.

Petraitis, J., Flay, B. R., & Miller, T. Q. (1995). Reviewing theories of adolescent substance use: Organizing pieces in the puzzle. *Psychological Bulletin, 117,* 67–86.

Shedler, J., & Block, J. (1990). Adolescent drug use and psychological health: A longitudinal inquiry. *American Psychologist, 45,* 612–630.

Sroufe, L. A. (1997). Psychopathology as an outcome of development. *Development and Psychopathology, 9,* 251–268.

Taylor, R. D, & Wang, M. C. (Eds.). (2000). *Resilience across contexts: Family, work, culture, and community.* Mahwah, NJ: Lawrence Erlbaum Associates, Inc.

Zimmer-Gembeck, M. J., Alexander, T., & Nystrom, R. J. (1997). Adolescents report their need for and use of health care services. *Journal of Adolescent Health, 21,* 388–399.

Ziv, A., Boulet, J. R., & Slap, G. B. (1999). Utilization of physician offices by adolescents in the United States. *Pediatrics, 104,* 35–42.

Applied Developmental Science
2006, Vol. 10, No. 2, 61–74

Observed Ecological Assets in Families, Schools, and Neighborhoods: Conceptualization, Measurement, and Relations With Positive and Negative Developmental Outcomes

Christina Theokas and Richard M. Lerner
Tufts University

The relations among observed ecological assets in youth's families, schools, and neighborhoods with positive and negative developmental outcomes were assessed with a sample of 646 fifth-grade youth. The majority of participants were Latino (37.5%) or European American (35.5%) and lived in 2-parent families. Ecological asset indicators were categorized into 4 dimensions: human, physical or institutional, collective activity, and accessibility and were measured equivalently across the three contexts. Different dimensions of the family, school, and neighborhood settings had the most comprehensive impact on the different developmental outcomes, specifically collective activity in the family, accessibility in school, and human resources in the neighborhood. This research establishes a baseline for the empirical inquiry into the impact of observed resources present within families, school, and neighborhoods.

Contemporary developmental science recognizes that human development is a bidirectional, individual ↔ context relational process (Lerner, 2006). Just as there are multiple levels of organization within the individual (e.g., genes, motivation, and cognitive abilities) that influence one's developmental course, so too are there different levels of organization within the social ecology (e.g., families, schools, and neighborhoods) that contribute to development. In this article, we focus on the multilevel social context. We propose a framework for conceptualizing and measuring different, observed aspects of the social ecology that can be simultaneously applied to multiple settings to examine the unique and combined effects of the ecology on positive and negative developmental outcomes.

Common Features of Positive Developmental Settings

Recent research has begun to specify the critical elements of social contexts important for positive youth development (PYD; Barber & Olsen, 1997; Benson, 2003; Eccles & Gootman, 2002; Gambone & Connell, 2004). These ideas have emerged from a long history of research on families and schools and, more recently, on neighborhoods. This research shares the assumption that young people are more likely to thrive when their developmental needs are matched with resources in the environment and when there is synergy between multiple settings. A key hypothesis of this work is that the more exposure a youth has to these resources and experiences, the more likely he or she will develop positively.

For instance, Barber and Olsen (1997) and Eccles, Early, Frasier, Belansky, and McCarthy (1997) proposed three basic experiences (i.e., connection, regulation, and autonomy) to define youth's main associations with their environment that can be measured across multiple settings (neighborhoods, schools, families, siblings, and peer groups). Findings across both studies indicated that if youth reported positive experiences in one setting (e.g., families), they were likely to also report positive experiences in the other contexts (e.g., peer groups). Furthermore, if youth reported positive interactions in regard to one socialization dimension (e.g., regulation), they were likely to also have positive interactions on the other two constructs (connection and autonomy). Positive experiences across the four settings added linearly and independently to the prediction of positive adolescent outcomes, with few statistical interactions noted (see also, Cook, Herman, Phillips, & Settersten, 2002).

Benson (2003) and colleagues at Search Institute (Benson, Leffert, Scales, & Blyth, 1998; Leffert et al., 1998; Scales et al., 2000) proposed slightly different ideal social experiences for youth. Their model includes four categories of what they term external assets: support, boundaries and expectations, empower-

---

This article is based on a dissertation submitted by Christina Theokas to Tufts University in partial fulfillment of the requirements for the Ph.D. degree. The research was supported in part by a grant from the National 4-H Council.

Correspondence should be directed to Christina Theokas, Child Trends, 4301 Connecticut Ave NW Suite 100, Washington, D.C. 20008. E-mail: ctheokas@childtrends.org

ment, and constructive use of time. Although their research does not examine the impact of specific contexts or distinguish the predictive power of categories of assets, their empirical findings test and support the notion that additive increases in the total number of self-reported, perceived ecological resources is positively related to higher levels of thriving behaviors and lower levels of risk behaviors.

Finally, two additional frameworks have been proposed. Eccles and Gootman (2002) articulated a provisional list of eight essential elements of positive developmental settings. They hypothesized that young people will develop positive personal and social assets in settings that have these eight features: physical and psychological safety; clear and consistent structure and appropriate supervision; supportive relationships; opportunities to belong; positive social norms; support for efficacy and mattering; opportunities for skill building; and integration of family, school, and community efforts. Similarly, Gambone and Connell (2004) specified five supports and opportunities that are critical in all settings for providing the building blocks of successful development. They include adequate nutrition, health, and shelter; multiple supportive relationships with adults and peers; challenging and engaging activities and learning experiences; meaningful opportunities for involvement and membership; and physical and emotional safety.

The work on optimal contexts of development advances research by focusing on youths' developmental needs, supports, and resources and considers multiple social contexts. Common indicators have been proposed for all social contexts (e.g., safety and supportive relationships). Moreover, there is agreement across multiple proposed frameworks. Empirical research has examined youths' perceived experiences within contexts and linked these experiences with key indicators of youth development. However, these models also all specify documentation of norms, resources for skill building, and engagement and integration of key contexts as essential components of positive developmental settings. For example, the availability of youth programs for skill building and group membership has not been measured and examined, although there is agreement that these actual resources are necessary for positive development and are often the targets of community organizing and policy intervention.

This research focuses on documenting these types of resources present in youth's families, schools, and neighborhoods. Structural and descriptive features of settings necessarily precede youth experiences (e.g., autonomy) in a setting. Without the availability of opportunities, no attempts can be made by youth to develop new skills or build meaningful and supportive relationships with caring adults. For example, without athletic fields or access to computers and books, youth cannot learn to play a sport, to use the Internet, or to read and learn about things of interest. This data, when combined with individual reports of their perceived experiences within social settings, will expand current knowledge about the impact of the ecology on PYD.

A Framework to Specify Features of the Actual Ecology

We attempt to define the dimensions into which resources in the actual ecology can be categorized. Past research has examined discrete aspects of families (e.g., family size), schools (e.g., type), and communities (e.g., percentage unemployed); the goal of this research is to propose major categories of observed ecological resources that are applicable to all settings and to assess the impact of those dimensions across multiple ecologies, much like connection, regulation, and autonomy are examined across contexts (e.g., Eccles et al., 1997).

The theoretical basis for the proposed asset categories emerges from community action models (e.g., Kretzmann & McNight, 1993), the neighborhood effects models specified by Leventhal and Brooks-Gunn (2000), forms of capital (Bordieu, 1983; Coleman, 1988), and models of optimal contexts for youth development (e.g., Eccles & Gootman, 2002). Each of these sources specifies the mechanisms or necessary conditions for positive development and for the promotion of positive social experiences. In particular, they converge in specifying that assets can be conceived of within individuals, in the physical space, and emerging in the dynamic between the two. Thus, four categories of observed ecological assets—human, physical or institutional, collective activity, and accessibility—are proposed to organize the actual resources and opportunities in the environments of youth. The asset categories are intended to represent broad areas of potential inputs and connectivity between youth and resources for positive developmental outcomes. As well, the indicators, within the dimensions, are measured separate from youth perceptions of social settings, which has been the focus of past research. Although individuals may report the status of an indicator (e.g., number of nights family has dinner together), it could also be externally observed and should not vary in relation to reporter characteristics.

The first key dimension of observed measures of ecological assets involves the individuals in the environment. Human resources are defined as the strengths, skills, talents, and abilities of people and as instantiated by the roles they have (Coleman, 1988; Kretzmann & McKnight, 1993). For example, individuals can model conventional behaviors, standards, and expectations (e.g., high school graduation) or can reflect maladaptive, unengaged citizenship (e.g., involvement with drug dealing). The characteristics, activities, and behaviors of individuals provide a manifestation of the social norms of a particular context.

The second dimension of actual ecological assets is the physical and institutional resources present in the social environment. These assets are intended to document opportunities for learning, recreation, and engagement with individuals and the physical world around oneself and, as well, for providing routines and structure for youth. For example, when families have medical and dental insurance, children and youth are regularly seen by physicians who monitor their physical health and well-being. These experiences become routine for children and youth and part of how they think about themselves and of how they view the procedures needed to address their (in this case physical) needs. Thus, the presence of these resources regulates experiences and opportunities for youth. One assumption is that proximity to resources (or presence of resources within the family) increases awareness, opportunity, and the likelihood of involvement. For example, at the neighborhood level, presence of libraries, community centers, and cultural experiences that are within walking distance, are drop off points on school bus routes, or are readily available through public transportation may increase their use and thus their potential benefits.

The third dimension of assets is collective activity. This asset dimension is intended to document mutual engagement between community members, parents, youth, school personnel, and institutions of society. These organizations, groups, or mutual activities represent the combined efforts and actions of different sets of individuals. In some cases, these coalitions symbolize group efforts for advocacy (e.g., a Parent Advisory Committee) or civic leadership (e.g., a neighborhood watch); in others they denote shared activity (e.g., family dinners). Documenting these relationships provides an understanding of the social ties and connections among community members. The primary bases for this component of the model derives from Coleman's (1988) notion of social capital and Sampson's (2001) ideas regarding collective efficacy. Social capital is the resource potential of social networks, and collective efficacy represents the activation of these networks for specific outcomes. Significant research has established a connection between social capital and youth outcomes (e.g., Sampson, Raudenbush, & Earls, 1997). Documenting ties and network is one way of establishing instances of a community's associational life and the climate of the key contexts of development.

The final dimension is accessibility. Similar to the dimension of collective activity, this category attempts to capture the dynamic between individuals and contexts. As such, this category is intended to document the ability of residents to partake of human resources and resource opportunities in the context. Accessibility can be conceptualized and operationalized in multiple ways. First, accessibility can refer to the transportation capacity and hours of operation of local businesses, infrastructure, or cultural institutions in a local community. This is a first level and documents physical ease of access. Second, accessibility can refer to the potential of youth to interact with the adults in the setting. For example, what is the ratio of adults to children in a given neighborhood or how long has a family lived in a neighborhood, so that local youth and adults can get to know one another? In this case, accessibility is ease of access of the human resources. Finally, accessibility can be conceived of in terms of the safety of the physical environment. It is perhaps the case that businesses and adults are accessible to youth; however, the physical environment must also be safe and free of dangers (e.g., crime) and promote the care and maintenance of the ecology (e.g., provision of rules in a family or community policing).

This Study

The data examined in this article are derived from the first wave (school year 2002–2003) of the 4-H Study of Positive Youth Development (Lerner et al., 2005). This study reports on a selected subsample of participants from the larger national study to pilot test the conceptual model of observed ecological assets. The sample was chosen to include various community types (e.g., urban, suburban, and rural) with diverse individual demographic characteristics to have a broad basis from which to test the proposed model. A full or ideal instantiation of the conceptual framework was not possible given that only certain indicators were available to be collected retrospectively. In particular, indicators at the family level were either reported by the youth or parent and were limited to those items included in the Wave 1 questionnaires. Indicators for school and neighborhood are collected from other reporters and governmental data sources (e.g., the U.S. Census). Nonetheless, each indicator matches the proposed definitions and is supported by previous research and practitioner wisdom about essential features of the social ecology.

The ecological asset indicators are summed to form composites representing the four dimensions of the model for each setting (families, schools, and neighborhoods) and examined in relation to both positive and negative developmental outcomes. Both types of outcomes are included to assess whether similar or different features of the ecology influence their development. A youth development framework supposes that investing in healthy development, by aligning resources in the ecology with developmental needs will lead to both a reduction in negative, risky behaviors, as well as the growth of functional, thriving behaviors; however this assumption has not been tested empirically. This manuscript includes two newly developed measures, specifically a PYD composite score and a measure of youth contribution (see Lerner et al., 2005), as well as two traditional indicators of problem behaviors, depression, and a combined measure of delinquency and substance use, for use as dependent variables.

Three key hypotheses are being tested in relation to the proposed conceptual dimensions: (a) All dimensions within settings are expected to have a positive impact on the outcomes, (b) more proximal settings are expected to account for greater amounts of variance, and (c) each dimension will add linearly and independently to the prediction of adolescent outcomes, as has been previously found (Eccles et al., 1997). No statistical interactions will be tested, as there is no literature guiding these decisions, and the focus of this article is to test the utility of the proposed model.

Method

Schools

Six school districts with their participating public schools (N = 17), youth (N = 646), and parents (N = 372) were chosen for inclusion in this study. These six districts were chosen from the larger study to represent different regions of the country (Northeast, Northwest, Southeast, Southwest) with unique demographic, population density, and land area characteristics that may vary in number and type of observed ecological resources. The total number of youth sampled in each school varied (average participation rate = 41%, range = 6% to 85%). Active consent was required for participation. All 5th graders were eligible if they returned consent prior to data collection and were English speaking. Table 1 presents key school characteristics and the percentage of participants in each category. All schools were public, coeducational schools, which varied in size, grades served, socioeconomic characteristics, and locale designation. All demographic data were collected from the National Center for Educational Statistics 2002–2003 school profiles. Participants were more likely to attend midsized, K–5 schools, but they were distributed throughout urban, suburban, and rural locations.

Participants

Youth participants were a diverse group of 646 fifth graders (M age = 11.06, SD = .51, 51% women, average mother's education = 13.3 years, average household income = $43,347). The majority of participants were Latino (37.5%) or European American (35.5%; African American, 7.6%; Asian American, 3.6%, Multiethnic, 5.2%; and other, 6%). The majority of youth came from two-parent families (70.7%).

Table 1. *School Characteristics*

	N	%	% Participants
School size			
Less than 400 students	3	18	14.2
401 to 800 students	8	47	48.5
More than 800 students	6	35	37.3
Grades served			
PK through 5	11	65	65.3
PK through 6	5	29	28.8
PK through 8	1	6	5.9
Non-European American			
0 to 25%	3	18	18.4
26 to 50%	2	12	9.8
51 to 75%	4	24	34.4
76 to 100%	8	47	37.5
Free and reduced lunch			
0 to 25%	3	18	24.3
26 to 50%	3	18	26.6
51 to 75%	1	6	12.2
76 to 100%	10	59	36.9
Locale			
Urban	7	41	38.2
Suburban	5	29	30.2
Rural	5	29	31.6

Data Collection

Youth and Parents

At all school sites, a 2-hr block of time was allotted for data collection during which the students were asked to complete a student questionnaire (SQ) developed for use in the 4-H Study of PYD (described in detail in Lerner et al., 2005). The SQ includes well-validated scales assessing psychological constructs, as well as items assessing youth activity engagement, behavioral choices, and expectations for the future. Guardians were sent a questionnaire with the consent documentation, which included items about the family and neighborhood, and were asked to send it back to the research staff in a self-addressed, postage-paid envelope.

Schools

Principals or a designated representative (e.g., other school administrators) completed a "School Survey" that included questions about the academic climate of the school, and as well the resources available at the school (e.g., playgrounds, academic tutors). Data were also collected from state departments of education online databases regarding mandated reporting items (e.g., years of experience of teachers).

Neighborhoods

This study defined the neighborhood unit of analysis as census tract. Participant's addresses were inputted into the American Fact Finder on the U.S. Census Web site (www.census.gov) to identify the census tract within which he or she lived. Number of participants per census tract varied widely from 1 to 50 depending on participants' proximity to their neighborhood school, land area characteristics, and population distribution. This division provided neighborhood asset scores at the individual level and focused on the immediate proximity of resources for the promotion of positive youth outcomes.

Documentation of resources followed multiple steps to determine their exact location and census tract. First, the 2000 Census reports were used to document key characteristics of the tract in which each student lived that were relevant to ecological assets. Second, city Web sites (e.g., www.ci.cityname.stateinitial.us/), county Web sites, as well as online directories (e.g., www.superpages.com/) were searched to document the presence of ecological assets within youths' neighborhoods. After resources were located with the various search engines, their addresses were input into the American Fact Finder and the exact census tract location identified.

Measures

Youth Outcomes

Positive developmental characteristics. Two variables are utilized as indicators of positive development. The first is a PYD composite score. Lerner et al. (2005) described in detail the specification and confirmation in LISREL of the latent factor measurement model of the "Five Cs" of competence, confidence, character, caring, and connection and of their convergence on a second order factor representing the PYD construct. The variable is a standard score, comprised of 17 well-validated scales assessing positive adolescent characteristics ($M = -.12$, $SD = .97$). The second composite is a measure of contribution. The construction of contribution followed a different methodology. The definition of contribution introduced by Lerner et al. suggested that there is both an ideological and a behavioral component to contribution. The ideology of contribution was obtained by coding responses to three open-ended questions assessing youths' definitions of a thriving individual. Responses that reflected a desire for or commitment to giving back to the world around them were coded as 0 (*absent*) or 1 (*present*). The behavioral component of contribution quantifies youth active participation—0 (*no involvement*) or 1 (*involvement*) more than once a month—in five different service oriented activities (being a leader in a group, being a peer mentor, helping friends and neighbors, participating in school government, and volunteering in the community). The eight items used to measure contribution were considered a variable set, and a sum score was computed ($M = 2.67$, $SD = 1.4$).

Negative developmental characteristics. Two measures that represent internalizing (depression) and externalizing (delinquency and substance use) problems were included as negative developmental indicators. Indicators of externalizing behavior were measured with a set of questions developed for this study. The questions were modified from items included in Profiles of Student Life: Attitudes and Behaviors Scale (Leffert et al., 1998) and the Monitoring the Future Questionnaire (Bachman, Johnston, & O'Malley, 2001). Five items assess the frequency of substance use (e.g., cigarettes, alcohol) in the last year. The response format ranges from 0 (*never*) to 3 (*regularly*). Four items assess the frequency of delinquent behaviors (e.g., trouble with the police). The response format ranges from 0 (*never*) to 4 (*5 or more times*). The nine items were standardized on a 12-point scale (Cronbach $\alpha = .73$) and a sum score was calculated for each youth measuring total engagement in risk behaviors ($M = 4.23$, $SD = 8.28$, range = 0 to 94). The incidence of risk behaviors is low in the sample, with the majority of youth not engaging in any (52%).

The Center for Epidemiological Studies Depression Scale (CES–D; Radloff, 1977) was used to assess depressive symptomatology. In this data set, the Cronbach alpha for this measure is .82. Youth responded to 20 items and reported how often they felt that way during the past week (e.g., sad). The response format ranged from 0 (*rarely/none of the time*) to 3 (*most/all of the time*). Items are summed for a total score ($M = 15.77$, $SD = 8.9$, range = 0 to 54).

Ecological Assets

Indicators were chosen for each dimension and setting in accordance with the definition proposed in this article. Some indicators are dichotomous, indicating the presence or absence of the resource; other indicators are measured on interval scales indicating the amount of the variable present.

Family variables. Documentation of family assets comes from the student and parent questionnaires. Although self-report, they are reports of data with an observable referent, as opposed to representing youths' perceptions of something that may vary due to perceiver characteristics. A single indicator was available for each domain of assets. Family assets present in the dataset include mother's years of school as an indicator of the human assets in the family ($M = 13.3$, $SD = 2.2$). In prior research, mother's education has proven to be a robust predictor of a child's status attainment in adulthood

(Featherman & Hauser, 1978). Household income is utilized as an indicator of the physical resource potential of a family (*M* = $43,347, *SD* = $27,239). As is the case with mother's education, research has documented the power of financial resources for a family, and numerous policies and programs (e.g., Welfare to Work) have been implemented to support the financial development of a family. Number of nights a family eats dinner together document collective activity of family members (*M* = 4.75, *SD* = 2.3). Number of adults in the home is used as the indicator of the accessibility of adults for youth (*M* = 2.0, *SD* = .80).

School variables. Multiple indicators were available for each dimension (see Table 2). As such, a composite is created for each dimension by standardizing (when necessary) and summing the individual indicators. Human assets are measured through the educational attainment and experience of the teachers (two indicators standardized and summed; *M* = .35, *SD* = 1.7). Physical or institutional resources are categorized into three areas, recreational (gym and outdoor fields), academic (tutors, enrichment programs, peer mentors), and extended day programs that may include opportunities for academic, sports, or dramatic arts programs. These resources represent opportunities for learning and engagement across different aspects of development, including academic, athletic, and artistic. Nine possible resources were identified and summed (*M* = 4.9, *SD* = 2.1). Collective activity documents the bidirectional interactions between schools and parents, that is, do schools prepare a newsletter to communicate with families (0 = *no*, 1 = *yes*) and the frequency of parental attendance at school events . The two indicators are standardized and summed (*M* = .34, *SD* = 1.4). Accessibility is measured through student–teacher ratio and overall school size, representing the potential of youth to develop relations with adults. The two indicators are standardized and summed (*M* = 0, *SD* = 1.7).

Neighborhood variables. Table 3 provides descriptive information for all indicators. Human assets are documented by educational attainment (percentage college educated residents), work status of adults (percentage employed adult men), and the presence of mentors in the youth's life. The three indicators were standardized and summed to form the human asset composite (*M* = 0, *SD* = 1.9). Physical or institutional resources fall into the same general categories as school resources, educational, recreational, and after-school time use. A total of seven institutional resources were summed (*M* = 2.0, *SD* = 1.1). Collective activity includes indicators of community organizing, with the presence (1) or absence (0) of a neighborhood group or youth coalition, for the betterment of the residents. The two indicators were summed (*M* = .70, *SD* =

Table 2. *Observed School Ecological Assets*

Indicator	Source of Items	Range	Item	*M*	*SD*
Human Resources					
Teacher education	NCLB Report Card	14.90 to 54.00	Percentage of teachers with master's degrees	39.34	9.7
Teacher experience	NCLB Report Card	6.30 to 15.70	Average years of experience of teachers	12.30	3.1
Physical Resources					
Recreation resources	Principal Q	0 to 2	(a) gym (b) outdoor playground or fields	1.67	.54
Academic resources	Principal Q	0 to 3	(a) academic tutors (b) enrichment programs (c) peer mentors	1.88	1.2
Afterschool programs	Principal Q	0 to 4	(a) clubs (b) sports (c) music (d) drama (e) theater	1.37	1.5
Collective Activity					
School communication	Principal Q	0 to 1	Parent newsletter	.86	.35
Parent participation	Principal Q	10 to 95	Average parental participation at school sponsored events	62.28	24.59
Accessibility					
Student teacher ratio	NCES	13.3 to 20.2	Number of full time teachers/total student enrollment	16.61	2.1
School size	NCES	351 to 1150	Total enrollment	667.76	256.7

Note: NCLB = No Child Left Behind; NCES = National Center for Education Statistics; Q = questionnaire.

Table 3. *Observed Neighborhood Ecological Assets*

Indicator	Source of Items	Range	Items	*M*	*SD*
Human Resources					
Education level	Census 2000	1 to 68	Percentage of college educated residents	21.61	1 7.6
Employment level	Census 2000	23 to 83	Percentage of employed adult males	65.41	1 4.5
Adult mentor	SQ	0 to 2	Youth has one or more adults to talk to if he or she has a problem	1.08	.58
Physical Resources					
Library	NCES	0 to 1	A local library	.10	.29
Youth facilities	Online	0 to 3	(a) Local youth center (b) Boys & Girls Club (c)YMCA	.59	.66
Recreation opportunities	Online	0 to 3	(a) City/town parks (b) State/national parks (c) Recreation program	1.33	.59
Collective Activity					
Neighborhood group	Online	0 to 1	An organization that represents the needs of the neighborhood	.17	.38
Youth coalition	Online	0 to 1	A local organization devoted to youth development and needs	.53	.49
Accessibility					
Neighborhood stability	Census 2000	21 to 79	Percentage of residents in neighborhood more than 5 years	48.34	1 0.6
Ratio adults to children	Census 2000	1.15 to 12.69		2.93	1.5

Note: SQ = student questionnaire; NCES = National Center for Education Statistics.

.70). Accessibility documents the availability of adults to youth with two indicators from the U.S. Census: neighborhood stability and the ratio of children to adults. The two indicators were standardized and summed to form a composite ($M = 0$, $SD = 1.4$).

Results

Correlational Analyses

The zero-order correlation matrix involving the 12 Dimension × Setting predictor variables and the positive and negative developmental outcome variables is presented in Table 4. The correlations were examined in multiple ways. First, they were examined for the consistency of access to human, physical or institutional, collective activity, and accessibility across the three key contexts of adolescent development. Across contexts, access to human resources was positive and significant, such that there was some tendency for all youth to experience similar types of human resources across settings. Physical resources were modestly related across settings. Physical resources between the family and school settings were more strongly related than between the family and neighborhood settings. Collective activity and accessibility across settings was not strongly related.

Next, the correlation matrix was inspected for within-context correlations among the observed ecological asset dimensions. Different relations were noted between the observed ecological asset dimensions within contexts. For example, in the family context, human and physical resources were positively related. This relation was expected as the indicators for these dimensions are educational attainment and household income. No other significant relations were noted in the family context. There were significant positive correlations between human resources and collective activity and accessibility, and between physical resources and collective activity in the school context. However, a strong, significant negative correlation existed between physical resources and accessibility in the school context, suggesting that larger schools have more physical resources in the forms of programs. In the neighborhood setting, accessibility was positively related to human and physical resources, suggesting communities that are more stable and have more adults are relatively more advantaged. Similarly, collective activity in the neighborhood was negatively related to human and physical resources and accessibility, indicating that com-

Table 4. *Interitem Correlations Among Predictor and Outcome Variables*

	1	2	3	4	5	6	7	8	9	10	11	12	13	14	15	16
1. Family: Human resources	—															
2. Family: Physical resources	.581**	—														
3. Family: Collective activity	.047	.052	—													
4. Family: Accessibility	-.050	.015	.027	—												
5. School: Human resources	.162**	.265**	-.007	-.057	—											
6. School: Physical resources	.374**	.334**	-.034	.020	-.036	—										
7. School: Collective activity	.396**	.418**	.102**	-.029	.703**	.267**	—									
8. School: Accessibility	-.349**	-.305	.079*	.022	.288**	.639**	.111**	—								
9. Nei: Human resources	.489**	.659**	.027	-.031	.400**	.306**	.493**	-.225**	—							
10. Nei: Physical resources	-.074	.089*	-.041	.069	-.082*	.063	-.199**	-.030	.010	—						
11. Nei: Collective activity	.089*	-.132**	.077	-.028	-.160**	.080*	.109**	-.110**	-.151**	-.502**	—					
12. Nei: Accessibility	.255**	.400**	-.033	-.077	.504**	.088*	.461**	-.060	.316**	.132**	-.286**	—				
13. Positive youth development	.157**	.186**	.330**	.042	.048	.099*	.175**	.049	.133**	-.044	-.029	.042	—			
14. Contribution	-.041	-.025	.081*	.035	.052	-.159**	.037	.227**	-.036	-.024	.008	-.006	.274**	—		
15. Depression	-.173**	-.234**	-.194**	-.026	-.120*	-.157**	-.217**	.045	-.210**	-.024	.011	-.047	-.481**	-.065	—	
16. Risk behaviors	-.086*	-.101*	-.112**	-.026	-.147**	-.056	-.192**	-.062	-.120**	.079*	.014	-.055	-.380**	-.075	.288**	—

Note: Nei = neighborhood.
$^{*}p < .05$. $^{**}p < .01$.

munity organizations are more likely to proliferate in more needy communities. These varied relations indicate substantial room for compensating (and conflicting) patterns of access to assets across these three contexts for the promotion of positive development.

Multivariate Analyses

Hierarchic multiple regression was used to assess the relation of human, physical or institutional, collective activity, and accessibility dimensions within the three key settings to the four indicators of adolescent development. The first step included demographic predictors (gender: 1 = *female*; race or ethnicity: 3 separate variables for European American, African American, and Latino; urbanicity: with higher numbers being more rural). Next, the Dimension × Setting scores were entered in sets from the most proximal context to the most distal context (i.e., family, school, neighborhood) to assess the amount of variance that was accounted for by each setting, while controlling for more proximal contexts. Specifically, the four dimension scores for the family were entered at Step two, the four scores for the school entered at Level 3, and the four neighborhood dimension scores entered at Step 4. Neighborhood scores were considered the most distal, due to the age (10- to 11-year-olds) and thus, restricted autonomy of participants. Further, by entering the family variables at Step two, household income and mother's education, which are also proxies for family socioeconomic status and are often key demographic control variables in research on adolescent outcomes, were controlled for when analyzing all other resources. This research attempted to go beyond the assumption that poverty and its correlates are the prime influences on development. Rather, each family, school, and neighborhood has resources that can be capitalized on to support the growth and development of adolescents. Regression analyses were conducted separately for each of the four criterion variables and are presented in Table 5.

Table 5. *Standardized Parameter Estimates, P Values, and Associated Goodness-of-Fit Statistics for OLS-Fitted Regression Models That Describe the Relation Between Observed Ecological Assets and Each of the Outcome Variables, Controlling for Sex, Race and Ethnicity, and Locale*

	PYD	Contribution	Depression	Risk Behaviors
Sex (1 = female)	.166***	.207***	−.022	−.205***
European American	.017	−.037	−.109*	−.022
Latino	.024	−.093	−.004	.012
African American	.005	−.009	.127**	.194***
Residential locale (rural)	.005	.076	.026	.054
F	6.19***	6.45***	4.41***	11.57***
df	620	620	620	620
ΔR^2	.05	.05	.03	.09
Family				
Human resources	.052	.047	−.050	−.018
Physical resources	.128**	.003	−.184***	−.080
Collective activity	.334***	.147**	−.190***	−.091**
Accessibility	.031	.022	−.023	−.016
F	16.06***	4.35***	8.83***	7.74***
df	616	616	616	616
ΔR^2	.14	.01	.08	.02
School				
Human resources	−.087	−.011	−.006	−.062
Physical resources	.177***	.056	−.137**	−.081
Collective activity	.024	.047	−.049	−.038
Accessibility	.235***	.222***	−.059	−.140**
F	12.74***	5.61***	6.93***	6.46***
df	612	612	612	612
ΔR^2	.02	.05	.02	.02
Neighborhood				
Human resources	.159***	.097*	−.058	−.030
Physical resources	−.068	.024	−.054	.084
Collective activity	−.078	.069	.044	.046
Accessibility	.030	.039	.110*	.015
F	10.92***	4.60***	5.79***	5.17***
df	608	608	608	608
ΔR^2	.02	.01	.01	.01

Note: OLS = ordinary least squares; PYD = positive youth development.
*$p < .05$. **$p < .01$. ***$p < .001$.

Control Variables

The individual demographic control variables accounted for 3% to 9% of the variance in the four regression analyses. The control variables accounted for the most amount of variance in risk behaviors (9%). Gender did not predict depression, but was significantly related to the other criterion variables. With the exception of risk behaviors, girls reported higher scores. Race or ethnicity of youth was a significant predictor for depression and risk behaviors. Specifically, African American ethnicity was positively related to depression and risk, although its effects were attenuated for depression with the inclusion of the additional observed ecological variables. European American ethnicity was negatively related to depression, with all effects attenuated after the inclusion of the observed ecological asset variables. Residential locale was not significant in any of the models.

PYD

Each of the stepwise models was significant. Inclusion of more distal contexts accounted for smaller portions of variance with the R^2 decreasing with each additional level of the context added. Inclusion of family variables added 14% to the amount of variance explained. Both collective activity and family physical resources were significant predictors. None of the other family variables were significant. Inclusion of the school observed ecological assets added only 2% of variance, but two of the indicators were significant. Accessibility in school was positive related to PYD, as were school physical resources. The four neighborhood predictors added approximately another 2% of variance explained. The only Dimension × Setting score that was significant was the human resource variable.

Contribution

Again, each of the models was significant, although the pattern that emerged was different than what was observed with the PYD composite. In particular, school observed ecological assets accounted for the largest portion of variance (5%), with the family and neighborhood contexts only accounting for 1% each. One indicator within each setting positively predicted contribution: specifically, family collective activity, school accessibility, and neighborhood human resources.

Depression

The observed ecological asset scores accounted for an additional 11% of variance, with the family setting accounting for 8% of the 11%. Two indicators, family physical resources and collective activity accounted for this difference. The school ecological asset composites added only 2% variance to the model and it was the physical resource dimension. One neighborhood dimension score, accessibility, was significantly related to depression, although in the opposite direction as expected. The additional amount of variance accounted for was quite small, approximately 1%.

Risk Behaviors

Inclusion of the 12 Dimension × Setting scores, over and above the individual demographic variables, accounted for approximately another 5% of variance in the risk behavior composite. This is the only case where the observed ecological asset variables accounted for less variance than the control variables. The two indicators accounting for this were family collective activity and school accessibility. This is the only case where no neighborhood setting composites were significant.

Summary of Findings

Table 6 summarizes the findings from the multiple regression analyses regarding the impact of the observed ecological assets on the positive and negative developmental outcome variables. Six of the 12 Dimension × Setting asset composites had a significant

Table 6. *Summary Matrix for Significant Findings From Multiple Context Regression Analyses*

	Human Resources	Physical Resources	Collective Activity	Accessibility
Family		PYD Depression	PYD Contribution Depression Risk behaviors	
School		PYD Depression		PYD Contribution Depression Risk behaviors
Neighborhood	PYD Contribution			Depression (–)

Note: PYD = positive youth development.

impact on at least one outcome variable. The ecological asset composites predicted both positive and negative developmental outcomes. Interestingly, family collective activity and school accessibility predicted all of the outcomes, family and school physical resources predicted both a positive (PYD) and negative outcome (depression), whereas neighborhood human resources only predicted the positive outcomes. The family setting accounted for the largest portion of variance for PYD and depression, whereas the school setting composites accounted for the largest portion of variance for contribution. The three ecological settings added negligible amounts of variance to the prediction of risk behaviors (1% to 2%). It is important to note that this finding may be due to the limited variance in the risk behavior composite.

Discussion

Shifting the focus from a traditional deficit and prevention approach to a strength building and promotion approach, developmental researchers have turned towards understanding what experiences, resources, and opportunities are critical for youth in their key ecological contexts (Gambone & Connell, 2004; Larson, Eccles, & Gootman, 2004). This work focused on actual ecological assets or positive features of the individuals, physical space of the ecology, and engagement between the two. This research augments the literature on youth's perceived ecological experiences to expand understanding of the potential impact of the contexts of development for the promotion of healthy functioning.

To document resources across the four proposed dimensions—human, physical/institutional, collective activity, and accessibility—in three key contexts of adolescent development—family, school, and neighborhood—indicators of observed ecological assets were collected from multiple sources and added to the 4-H Study of Positive Youth Development existing dataset (Lerner et al., 2005). A full or ideal instantiation of the framework was not possible given that only certain indicators were available to work in conjunction with the 4-H dataset. However, the resources present allow for a discussion of the utility of the proposed dimensions across different contexts and as well of the simultaneous examination of their effects.

Despite the potential shortcomings of the data collection method and diverse circumstances of youth in the sample, several interesting findings emerged. Four major conclusions can be drawn from the results:

1. The proposed categorical dimensions are useful and each dimension, in at least one setting, predicted the developmental outcomes.
2. Different dimensions of the family, school, and neighborhood settings had the most comprehensive impact on the developmental outcomes, specifically collective activity in the family, accessibility in school, and human resources in the neighborhood.
3. Contrary to Hypothesis 2, it was not the case that more proximal contexts always accounted for larger amounts of variance in the outcomes, although the neighborhood composite scores consistently accounted for the smallest amounts of variance.
4. Observed ecological resources predicted both positive and negative developmental outcomes, providing some support that promoting positive development through the provision of resources is related to fewer negative developmental outcomes.

No specific relation was predicted among the four dimensions of observed ecological assets and the four developmental outcomes. All ecological asset dimensions were hypothesized to have a positive impact. Overall, no clear pattern emerged suggesting that a particular dimension, across settings, is related to a particular adolescent characteristic or that the combined resources of a particular setting were more strongly related to a particular outcome. Interestingly, unique dimensions within each setting were related to the outcomes. The physical resource dimension was the only dimension that was predictive in two settings, specifically families and schools. In these two cases, physical resources predicted both higher levels of PYD and lower levels of depression. Interestingly, availability of neighborhood physical institutional resources is conceptualized as a primary mechanism regarding the influence of neighborhoods on adolescent development, but in this study was not significantly related to the outcome variables (Leventhal & Brooks-Gunn, 2000). The learning, recreational, and social opportunities, along with child care, medical facilities, and employment opportunities provided by programs and community institutions are expected to create experiences that support the development of youth. Little empirical research has documented the actual presence or absence of resources in the community and their resulting impact on development. However field studies and ethnographic descriptions of neighborhoods have provided persuasive accounts of the experiences of individuals in resource restricted settings (Burton, 1990; MacLeod, 1987). Documenting the presence of resources may not be enough to assess their impact, as was done in this study. Perhaps adding youth reports of their engagement to indexes of these services and programs may yield more meaningful findings. Or, alternatively neighborhood physical resources may need to be measured differently.

One finding was in contrast to what was expected, a negative relation was found between neighborhood accessibility and depression. It could be that residential stability and a greater adult–youth ratio, although generally considered positive can also be negative. Specifically, residential stability can arise from individuals being trapped in economically disadvantaged situations which may have negative consequences on psychological functioning. Similarly, although there may be many adults available to youth, if they are not actively involved with youth or perceive youth negatively, it could have a detrimental effect on adolescent functioning. This counterintuitive finding points to the fact that maybe sometimes what we think in principle is good, is not necessarily always so. In research, it is important to examine these differences so we can understand the multiple pathways to positive development and how certain features of settings may interact with or counterbalance other features, or may only be positive in certain circumstances for specific groups of youth.

As well, although this research did not focus on individual differences, the individual demographic characteristics that were included as control variables yielded interesting finding. The model of thriving on which this research is based (Lerner, 2004) suggests that individual characteristics when aligned with ecological supports or assets promote healthy developmental regulations. Consistent with that idea, gender was significantly related to three of the four outcome variables. The only variable that gender did not impact was depression. In this sample, girls reported higher scores on the positive developmental outcomes and lower scores on delinquency. This finding is consistent with the perceived ecological assets literature (Theokas et al., 2005). Given the strength and consistency of this finding across both literatures, future research should examine findings separately by gender. It may be the case that girls experience their environments in consistently different ways, and indeed this difference may be reflected in different observed ecological asset dimensions and contexts having differential effects with girls and boys.

The race and ethnicity variable was only significant in the final model for delinquency. In this case, African American ethnicity was positively related to delinquency. No other relations were noted. However there may be an interaction between race and ethnicity and location of participants that can further elucidate this relationship. Indeed, future research may want to examine observed ecological assets separately for race and ethnicity and locale type. Prior research has demonstrated that youth in the United States grow up in significantly different cultural and economic circumstances (McLoyd, 1998). As well, delinquent behaviors, in general, are low in this sample. It will be important to monitor changes in these behaviors over time and their relation with ecological assets and as well ecological liabilities.

Finally, although not entered at step one in the hierarchic regression models, family socioeconomic indicators were included in all analyses at Step 2. Mother's education and household income were proxy indicators for family human and physical resources. Family human resources were not related to any of the outcome variables, whereas family physical resources were related to PYD and depression. The lack of a pervasive impact of these variables is noteworthy. It is perhaps the case that these variables indirectly impact the outcome variables as they are mediated by other process variables, such as parenting style (Conger et al., 1992; Elder, Eccles, Ardelt, & Lord, 1995). However, in this research, other observed ecological assets had more of a predictive relation with the various outcome variables (e.g., collective activity in families). A similar relation was noted in an empirical test of the predictive ability of perceived ecological assets for individual thriving behaviors (Theokas et al., 2005). Demographic control variables accounted for only 1% to 2% of the variance in the positive outcome variables (e.g., grades in school, helping others).

Conclusions and Future Directions

In sum, this research establishes a baseline for the empirical inquiry into the impact of observed resources present within families, schools, and neighborhoods. The hypothesis tested was that resources can be meaningfully categorized into four unique dimensions and that these dimensions can be usefully applied to understand the strengths of multiple contexts of development simultaneously. The findings demonstrate the utility of this model. However, there are key next steps to take to further this line of research. First, it is important to understand the relation between perceived and observed ecological assets both substantively and methodologically. Research has now demonstrated that both are useful and predictive of positive developmental outcomes. Common wisdom also suggests this is the case. Youth need both concrete opportunities for engagement and learning, synergy between key contexts of development, as well as experiences with others that provide support, monitoring, and expectations.

In addition, another key step would be to examine the data longitudinally to be able to model causality in a manner that was not possible with only one wave of data. Does the presence of observed assets predict different developmental trajectories over time? In this data, given the age of the participants, most youth reported feeling positively about themselves and few were engaging in negative behaviors. With both new challenges and opportunities as they move further into adolescence, the presence of assets may lead to different paths for youth. For example, although neighborhood physical resources had no impact in Wave 1, access to educational, recreational, and civic opportunities may become increasingly important as the identities of youth crystallize and they begin to make more choices regarding their interests and future.

Furthermore, the experiences youth have had or witnessed with their peers may have a cumulative impact thereby better preparing youth for new challenges later in adolescence.

Moreover, the set of indicators used in the present research was in part constrained by the characteristics of the method of the 4-H Study. Accordingly, additional indicators of ecological resources for PYD should be added to independently collected datasets in order to cross-validate and to extend examination of the present model.

Last, given the richness and breadth of the dataset, patterns of individual differences could be explored. These findings point towards specifically examining if the impact of observed ecological assets differs by gender and by locale type (rural–urban). By including all locale types in this study, the effects of certain indicators may have been washed away. Locale type may also interact with the economic realities of a particular setting. Similarly, the two sexes may be more or less responsive to particular dimensions of observed ecological assets. To date, research on the role of assets for youth development has assumed a somewhat universal and additive impact of assets for adolescent development (Benson, Scales, Hamilton, & Sesma, 2006). However, the theory guiding this research clearly specifies that there are multiple paths to positive outcomes and it is the imperative for developmental researchers to identify the unique strengths of individuals, families, and communities that can be capitalized on and aligned to promote thriving and healthy development.

References

Bachman, J. G., Johnston, J. D., & O'Malley, P. M. (2001). *Monitoring the future: Questionnaire responses from the nation's high school seniors, 2000.* Ann Arbor, MI: Institute for Social Research.

Barber, B. K., & Olsen, J. A. (1997). Socialization in context: Connection, regulation, and autonomy in the family, school, and neighborhood, and with peers. *Journal of Adolescent Research, 12*(2), 287–315.

Benson, P. L. (2003). Developmental assets and asset building communities: Conceptual and empirical foundations. In R. M. Lerner & P. L. Benson (Eds.), *Developmental assets and asset-building communities: Implications for research, policy, and practice* (pp. 19–43). Norwell, MA: Kluwer Academic.

Benson, P. L., Leffert, N., Scales, P. C., & Blyth, D. A. (1998). Beyond the "village" rhetoric: Creating healthy communities for children and adolescents. *Applied Developmental Science, 2*(3), 138–159.

Benson, P. L., Scales, P. C., Hamilton, S. F., & Sesma, A. (2006). Positive youth development: Theory, research and application. In R. M. Lerner (Vol. Ed.), *Theoretical models of human development. Volume 1 Handbook of Child Psychology* (6th ed., pp. 894–941). New York: Wiley.

Bordieu, P. (1983). Forms of capital. In J. C. Richards (Ed.) *Handbook of Theory and Research for the Sociology of Education* (pp. 241–258). New York: Greenwood Press.

Burton, L. (1990). Teenage childbearing as an alternative life-course strategy in multigenerational black families. *Human Nature, 1,* 123–143.

Coleman, J. S. (1988). Social capital in the creation of human capital. *American Journal of Sociology, 94,* S95–S120.

Conger, R. D., Conger, K. J., Elder, G. H., Lorenz, F. O., Simons, R. L., & Whitbeck, L. B. (1992). A family process model of economic hardship and adjustment of early adolescent boys. *Child Development, 63,* 527–541.

Cook, T. D., Herman, M., Phillips, M., & Settersten, R. A. (2002). Some ways in which neighborhoods, nuclear families, friendship groups, and schools jointly affect changes in early adolescent development. *Child Development, 73*(4), 1283–1309.

Eccles, J. S., Early, D., Frasier, K., Belansky, E., & McCarthy, K. (1997). The relation of connection, regulation, and support for autonomy to adolescents' functioning. *Journal of Adolescent Research, 12*(2), 263–286.

Eccles, J. S., & Gootman, J. A. (Eds.). (2002). *Community programs to promote youth development.* Washington, DC: National Academy Press.

Elder, G. H., Eccles, J. S., Ardelt, M., & Lord, S. (1995). Inner-city parents under economic pressure: Perspectives on the strategies of parenting. *Journal of Marriage and the Family, 57,* 771–784.

Featherman, D. L., & Hauser, R. K. (1978). *Opportunity and change.* New York: Academic.

Gambone, M. A., & Connell, J. P. (2004). The community action framework for youth development. *The Prevention Researcher, 11*(2), 6–10.

Kretzmann, J. P., & McKnight, J. L. (1993). *Building communities from the inside out: A path toward finding and mobilizing a community's assets.* Evanston, IL: Northwestern University, Center for Urban Affairs and Policy Research.

Larson, R., Eccles, J., & Gootman, J. A. (2004). Features of positive developmental settings. *The Prevention Researcher, 11*(2), 8–12.

Leffert, N., Benson, P. L., Scales, P. C., Sharma, A. R., Drake, D. R., & Blyth, D. A. (1998). Developmental assets: Measurement and prediction of risk behaviors among adolescents. *Applied Developmental Science, 2*(4), 209–230.

Lerner, R. M. (2004). *Liberty: Thriving and civic engagement among America's youth.* Thousand Oaks, CA: Sage.

Lerner, R. M. (2006). Developmental science, developmental systems, and contemporary theories of human development. In R. M. Lerner (Vol. Ed.), *Theoretical models of human development. Volume 1 of Handbook of Child Psychology* (6th ed., pp. 1–17). New York: Wiley.

Lerner, R. M., Lerner, J. V., Almerigi, J., Theokas, C., Phelps, E., Gestsdottir, S., et al. (2005). Positive youth development, participation in community youth development programs, and community contributions of fifth grade adolescents: Findings from the first wave of the 4-H Study of Positive Youth Development. *Journal of Early Adolescence, 25*(1), 17–71.

Leventhal, T., & Brooks-Gunn, J. (2000). The neighborhoods they live in: The effects of neighborhood residence on child and adolescent outcomes. *Psychological Bulletin, 126*(2), 309–337.

MacLeod, J. (1987). *Ain't no making it: Leveled aspirations in a low-income neighborhood.* Boulder, CO: Westview Press.

McLoyd, V. C. (1998). Socioeconomic disadvantage and child development. *American Psychologist, 53,* 185–204

Radloff, L. S. (1977). The CES-D scale: A self-report depression scale for research in the general population. *Applied Psychological Measurement, 1,* 385–401.

Sampson, R. J. (2001). How do communities undergird or undermine human development? Relevant contexts and social mechanisms. In A. Booth & A. C. Crouter (Eds.), *Does it take a village? Community effects on children, adolescents, and families* (pp. 3–30) . Mahwah, NJ: Lawrence Erlbaum Associates, Inc.

Sampson, R. J., Raudenbush, S., & Earls, F. (1997). Neighborhoods and violent crime: A multilevel study of collective efficacy. *Science, 277,* 918–924.

Scales, P. C., Benson, P. L., Leffert, N., & Blyth, D. A. (2000). The contribution of developmental assets to the prediction of thriving among adolescents. *Applied Developmental Science, 4,* 27–46.

Theokas, C., Almerigi, J., Lerner, R. M., Dowling, E., Benson, P., Scales, P. C., et al. (2005). Conceptualizing and modeling individual and ecological asset components of thriving in early adolescence. *Journal of Early Adolescence, 25*(1), *113–143.*

Received September 15, 2005
Final revision received October 19, 2005
Accepted October 19, 2005

Applied Developmental Science
2006, Vol. 10, No. 2, 75–85

A Longitudinal Examination of Family, Friend, and Media Influences on Competent Versus Problem Behaviors Among Urban Minority Youth

Julia A. Graber
University of Florida

Tracy Nichols
Weill Medical College, Cornell University

Sarah D. Lynne
University of Florida

Jeanne Brooks-Gunn
Columbia University

Gilbert J. Botvin
Weill Medical College, Cornell University

This article examines family, friend, and media influences on competent and problem behaviors in a sample of 1,174 urban minority youth followed over 6th, 7th, and 8th grades. Students completed annual surveys at their schools. Each of the contextual factors investigated was significantly associated with concurrent aggression and delinquency as well as changes in these outcomes over time. In contrast, parental monitoring was most often significantly associated with indicators of competence both concurrently and over time (e.g., from 7th to 8th grade). In addition, engagement with violent media contributed to decreases in academic achievement. Overall, findings indicate that family factors, specifically parental monitoring, as a target of intervention, would not only offset risk trajectories but enhance positive development.

The entry into adolescence has been linked to increases in problem behaviors such as delinquent and aggressive behaviors, as well as decreases in factors associated with competence (e.g., grades in school, self-esteem). Developmental psychopathology approaches suggest that the development of both positive and negative trajectories must be understood in order to identify potential targets for prevention and intervention via decreases in undesirable behaviors and promotion of desirable outcomes (e.g., Cicchetti & Cohen, 1995; Cummings, Davies, & Campbell, 2000; Masten & Curtis, 2000). These approaches also suggest that multiple contextual factors influence both competent and risky developmental trajectories. Previous studies have mainly focused on risky outcomes and therefore do not fully address how competent trajectories can be enhanced or whether contextual factors influence competent versus risky developmental pathways in the same manner. In this investigation, we focus on two commonly studied problem behaviors, aggression and delinquency, and three behaviors indicative of competence, school achievement (as tapped by grades), self-esteem, and assertiveness. We also identified a construct from each of three different contexts (family, peer, and media) that have been identified as salient to the development of problem behaviors and, to a lesser extent, to the development of competence. Our goal was to examine the role of these contextual factors on the development of problem and competent behaviors during early adolescence.

Although overall rates of aggressive and delinquent behaviors are higher in men than women, an increase in rates occurs for both genders during adolescence (Coie & Dodge, 1998). Moreover, in the past 20 years, while rates of some delinquent behaviors have decreased, rates of other behaviors (e.g., simple assault) have increased (Snyder, 2003). Although it has been argued that much of this behavior is potentially characteristic of the adolescent period and will desist once adult transitions are made (Moffitt, 1993), other evidence suggests that these behavioral patterns continue into adulthood and are a factor in successful adult role attainment (Farrington, 2004; Pajer, 1998). As such, adolescent aggression and delinquency may be part of a pathway for longer term psychopathology. Numer-

This project was supported in part by a grant to Gilbert J. Botvin, Ph.D., from the National Institute on Drug Abuse (P50DA-07656).

Correspondence should be sent to Julia A. Graber, Ph.D., Department of Psychology, University of Florida, P.O. Box 112250, Gainesville, FL 32611–2250. E-mail: jagraber@ufl.edu

ous studies, prevention programs, and policy debates have been undertaken with the goal of offsetting or preventing initiation of these trajectories with attention to individual and contextual factors that may serve as the targets of intervention. However, fewer studies have considered how such contextual factors may also be associated with the development of competence.

Competence has been defined as successfully meeting the challenges that occur across development and demonstrating the adaptational processes or skills that are needed to meet new and changing developmental demands (e.g., Catalano, Hawkins, Berglund, Pollard, & Arthur, 2002; Masten & Curtis, 2000). One approach to competence has been to focus on behavioral competence, often as the absence of problems rather than actual competence. In this investigation, we have attempted to separate these issues by looking at problem behaviors and indicators of competence as distinct constructs. In the domain of behavioral competence, prior studies of children and adolescents have identified competence in school, specifically academic achievement, as an important indicator of competence (e.g., Masten et al., 1995). Academic achievement has been identified as an indicator of how well a child or adolescent is doing in the school domain and as an indicator of a pathway for competence in adulthood (e.g., Ianni & Orr, 1996; Masten et al., 1995). However, academic achievement as assessed by grades in school often declines during the middle school years (Simmons & Blyth, 1987).

At the same time, to understand competence across domains, it is necessary to identify other indicators of successful adaptation to developmental demands. Self esteem is another commonly studied aspect of competence (see Baumeister, Campbell, Krueger, & Vohs, 2003; Harter, 1999). In general, positive self-evaluation should occur when individuals have attained competence in various domains and have the sense that they are capable of meeting developmental challenges. However, self esteem decreases during early and midadolescence for many adolescents (e.g., Simmons & Blyth, 1987). Potentially, lower self esteem is due to problems in developing competence or successful adaptation to the multiple challenges occurring at this time.

In the social domain, a skill that has been identified as critical for success is the ability to act assertively (e.g., Englander-Golden, Elconin, & Satir, 1986; Wills, Baker, & Botvin, 1989). Assertiveness is a broad, multidimensional construct that includes a variety of behaviors, expressed both verbally and nonverbally, that may be more or less effective and appropriate depending on several contextual factors. Assertive behavior that is typically expressed verbally includes making requests and refusing unwanted requests; expressing feelings (i.e., love and anger) and opinions, especially contrary opinions; and initiating friendship and dating relationships (Galassi & Galassi, 1978; Wills et al., 1989). In particular, several programs designed to prevent health compromising behaviors such as drug use or violence, seek to enhance assertive behaviors in order to combat peer pressure to engage in such behaviors or conformity to peer group norms. At the same time, few studies have focused on identifying factors associated with the development of assertiveness.

Contextual Factors That May Influence Problem Behaviors and Competence

A common assumption is that parental influences decrease during adolescence and peers and media become increasingly salient to shaping behavior. In particular, association with peers who are engaging in delinquent behaviors has commonly been identified as a risk factor for entering onto a pathway for delinquency and aggression (e.g., Moffitt, Caspi, Rutter, & Silva, 2001). Of course, selection biases have also been identified with youth who engage in delinquent behaviors being likely to seek out delinquent peers (Farrington, 2004). Attention has also focused on the role of media in influencing adolescent behavior (e.g., Brown & Cantor, 2000). Just as time spent with peers increases during adolescence, media use becomes more varied and increases during early adolescence (Roberts, Henriksen, & Foehr, 2004). In particular, engagement with violent media has been identified as a factor in the development of aggression (see Roberts et al., 2004, for a review).

Despite the salience of peers, especially deviant peers, and media influences, studies frequently find that familial contexts continue to be important influences on adolescents but that the relative roles of different contextual influences vary by the construct under investigation (i.e., parents tend to have more influence over career goals and academic achievement relative to peers, but peers may have greater impact on social activities and hence problem behaviors). In studies of behaviors, a parental factor that seems to be particularly salient to offsetting risk trajectories is parental monitoring; that is, parents who know what their adolescents are doing and who they are with are more likely to have adolescents who are not getting into trouble (e.g., Griffin, Botvin, Scheier, Diaz, & Miller, 2000). Most of the research has focused on how these contextual factors influence the development of problem behavior trajectories. Less is know about how each of these factors influences the development of competence during adolescence.

This article examined family, friend, and media influences on competent and problem behaviors in a sample of urban minority youth followed over 6th, 7th, and 8th grades. The study examined two main questions: (a) Are parental monitoring, friend delinquency, and engagement with violent media associated with problem or competent behaviors concurrently at the beginning of the middle school years in 6th grade? (b) Do the same or different contextual factors influence change in each of these behaviors over the course of middle school?

Method

Participants

Participants were 1,174 young adolescents drawn from the control condition of a larger randomized clinical trial targeting prevention of violence and aggression (see discussion of attrition later). In 6th grade, the mean age for this sample was 11.63 (*SD* = .47), 53.7% of the students were girls, and most of the students (83.1%) attended public school. Nearly half of the students were Black or African American (48%) with other racial or ethnic groups including Latino or Hispanic (27.9%), Asian (6.4%), Caucasian (7.6%) and biracial or "Other" (10.1%). Nearly half of the students came from an intact family (49.7%), 27.9% lived with a single parent, 12.8% lived in blended families (with stepparents or split time between mother's and father's homes), and the remainder (5.9%) lived in households without any parent present (with other relatives, or with foster parents or guardians). Although a measure of family socioeconomic status was not available, archival public school records of participating schools showed that the majority (88%) of schools had greater than 65% student eligibility for free or reduced lunch.

Procedure

A passive consent procedure approved by Weill Cornell Medical College's Institutional Review Board was used to inform parents about the nature of the study and to provide them with an opportunity to disallow their child's participation. A consent form describing the adolescent survey and the focus of the larger study was distributed in the schools for students to take home to their parents, as well as mailed directly to students' homes. Students (5%) whose parents indicated they did not want them to participate did not complete any of the data collection activities.

The survey was divided into two booklets, and data collection was conducted on two separate days during regular 40-min class periods. A multiethnic team of three to five data collectors administered the questionnaire following a standardized protocol similar to those used in previous research (e.g., Botvin, Schinke, Epstein, & Diaz, 1994). Identification codes rather than names were used to emphasize the confidential nature of the questionnaire, and students were assured about the confidentiality of their responses. Carbon monoxide breath samples were also collected at each annual survey assessment to enhance the validity of self-report data utilizing a variant of the bogus pipeline procedure (Evans, Hansen, & Mittlemark, 1977). Although this measure was used to increase the validity of questions pertaining to cigarette smoking, studies have shown bogus pipeline procedures can also increase the validity of other problem behaviors (Tourangeau, Smith, & Rasinski, 1997).

Measures

Competence and Problem Behavior Outcomes

Delinquency (past year). Students reported how many times in the past year they had engaged in each of 10 delinquent behaviors in 6th grade (α = .84), 7th grade (α = .87), and 8th grade (α = .89). The items were from a commonly used delinquency scale (Elliot, Huizinga, & Menard, 1989) that tapped behaviors such as violence, vandalism, and theft. Response categories were on a 5-point scale ranging from 1 (*never*), 2 (*once*), 3 (*2 to 3 times*), 4 (*4 to 5 times*), and 5 (*more than 5 times*). Items were rescored onto a scale of 0 to 4 and then summed to create a continuous measure where higher scores indicated greater number of delinquent behaviors in the past year.

Aggression (past month). Ten items from the aggression scale of the Youth Self-Report (Achenbach & Edelbrock, 1986) were used to assess general aggression in the 6th grade (α = .92), 7th grade (α = .93), and 8th grade (α = .94). Students were asked how many times in the past month they had engaged in each of ten overtly aggressive behaviors. Response categories were on a 5-point scale from 1 (*never*), 2 (*once*), 3 (*2 to 3 times*), 4 (*4 to 5 times*), and 5 (*more than 5 times*). Items were rescored onto a scale of 0 to 4 and then summed to create a continuous measure where higher scores indicated more aggressive behaviors.

Academic achievement. Students reported the grades they generally received in school, with response options ranging from 1 (*mostly As; 90–100*), to 5 (*Ds or lower; 60 or lower*). The item was reverse coded so that higher scores indicated better performance in school.

Self esteem. Five items (α = .86 in 6th grade, α = .90 in 7th grade, α = .91 in 8th grade) from Rosenberg's (1965) Self-Esteem Scale were used to assess global self-worth in each of the annual surveys. Response categories ranged from 1 (*strongly disagree*) to 5 (*strongly agree*). The mean of the items was calculated with higher scores reflecting higher self-esteem.

Assertion. Assertiveness was assessed annually using nine items ($\alpha = .68$ in 6th grade, $\alpha = .74$ in 7th grade, $\alpha = .78$ in 8th grade) from the Assertion Inventory (Gambrill & Richey, 1975). Each item had the common stem of "How likely would you be to do the following ... ?" and items included "say 'no' to someone who wants to copy your homework," and "ask someone for a favor." Responses were on a 5-point scale from 1 (*definitely would*) to 5 (*definitely would not*). Items were reverse coded and averaged with higher scores reflecting more assertiveness.

Contextual Influences

Parental monitoring. A 5-item scale ($\alpha = .75$ in 6th grade, $\alpha = .77$ in 7th grade, $\alpha = .81$ in 8th grade) assessing adolescents' perceptions that parents monitored their activities was taken from the Family Management scale (Catalano, Hawkins, Berglund, Pollard, & Arthur, 1993). Items included "My parent(s) know where I am when school is over," "My parent(s) know who I am with when I'm spending time with my friends," and so on. Response categories were on a 5-point Likert-type scale from 1 (*never*) to 5 (*always*). Items were averaged with higher scores indicating more monitoring.

Friends' delinquency (past year). Students were asked to indicate how many of their friends had engaged in each of seven delinquent behaviors in the past year in the 6th grade ($\alpha = .87$), 7th grade ($\alpha = .91$), and 8th grade ($\alpha = .92$). Items were taken from a scale developed by Elliot et al. (1989). Response categories were on a 5-point scale. Response options included 1 (*none*), 2 (*less than half*), 3 (*about half*), 4 (*more than half*), and 5 (*all or almost all*). Items were rescored onto a scale of 0 to 4 and then summed to create a continuous measure where higher scores indicated associating with more friends who engage in a higher number of delinquent behaviors for each time point.

Engagement with violent media. A 6-item scale ($\alpha = .71$ in 6th grade, $\alpha = .71$ in 7th grade, $\alpha = .71$ in 8th grade) assessing adolescents' engagement with violent media was developed for use in the larger clinical trial. Adolescents indicated how often they did each activity on a 5-point Likert-type scale from 1 (*never*) to 5 (*always*). Individual items included "Listen to 'Gangsta' rap," "Watch violent movies," and "Play video games that include killing (i.e., Mortal Kombat)." Items were averaged; higher scores indicated more engagement with violent media.

Demographic Variables

Students reported gender (1 = *male*, 0 = *female*), ethnicity, and household structure using standard survey items. Ethnicity was collapsed into 4 groups: (a) Black or African American, (b) Latino, (c) Caucasian and Asian, (d) and other. For analyses, 3 dummy coded variables were used with Black as the omitted group. Household structure was collapsed into two groups with *1* indicating living with two parents versus all other types. Because this variable changed across years, household structure was assessed from each survey. In 6th grade 61.4% of students lived in a two-parent household, in 7th grade 58.6%, and in 8th grade 57.7%. In addition, a variable for school type (1 = *public* vs. 0 = *parochial*) was created.

Attrition Analyses

At the first assessment in 6th grade, 2,931 students participated in the control condition of the larger study. From 6th to 7th grade, 5% of the sample was lost to attrition with an additional 31% lost between 7th and 8th grades. At each grade, between 2% and 30% of students did not complete both booklets of the survey. Thus, the maximum number of students with complete data was used in each of the following analyses resulting in a longitudinal sample of 1,174. Analyses of attrition bias were conducted to test for differences in 6th grade between students in this study and those who were dropped from any of the following analyses (*t* tests for continuous variables, χ^2 tests on background variables). Significantly fewer boys, $\chi^2(1, N = 2889) = 3.68$, $p = .030$, were retained in the longitudinal sample in comparison to the full sample (46.7% vs. 49.5%, respectively) and significantly fewer Latino, $\chi^2(3, N = 2912) = 14.77$, $p = .002$, students were in the final (25.8%) versus full sample (29.3%). Significantly more parochial school students, χ^2 $(1, N = 2931) = 180.60$, $p < .001$, were retained in the longitudinal (22.5%) versus full sample (10.5%) and significantly more students from two parent homes, $\chi^2(1, N = 2882) = 22.11$, $p < .001$, were in the final (63.3%) versus full sample (56.5%). Also, students who were maintained in all analyses reported significantly lower delinquency ($M = 3.50$ vs. $M = 3.96$), lower engagement with violent media ($M = 3.17$ vs. $M = 3.28$), higher levels of assertiveness ($M = 4.19$ vs. $M = 4.10$), higher levels of self-esteem ($M = 4.20$ vs. $M = 4.03$), and higher self-reported grades ($M = 3.98$ vs. $M = 3.65$). There were no significant differences found regarding aggression, association with delinquent friends, or parental monitoring.

Analysis Plan

Separate hierarchical regression analyses were conducted to examine the association of the contextual factors with concurrent problem behaviors and indicators of competence in 6th grade. Analyses controlled for race and ethnicity, school type, gender, and household structure on the first step. Contextual factors were entered on the second step. Two sets of longitudinal analyses (6th to 7th grade, 7th to 8th grade) were conducted in order to examine whether contextual factors predicted change in the problem behaviors and indicators of competence over time. In these analyses, the outcome variable from the prior time point was entered on the first step, and covariates were entered on the second step. Because household structure changed over time, household structure from the prior time point was entered on this step. Contextual factors from the prior time point were then entered on the last step.

Results

The means and standard deviations for the core variables are reported in Table 1. A series of repeated measures analyses (controlling for race and ethnicity, school type, gender, and household structure) were conducted to test for mean changes over time for each of the key constructs used in analyses; repeated *F* statistics and effect sizes are also reported in Table 1. As can be seen, in 6th grade, young adolescents reported on average having engaged in just over 3 delinquent behaviors in the past year and several aggressive behaviors in the past month (M = 11.96). Furthermore, delinquent behaviors and aggression significantly increased across 6th, 7th, and 8th grades.

Turning to the indicators of competence, in 6th grade, young adolescents reported receiving mostly *B*s and *C*s on average (M = 3.91); grades in school did not change significantly over time. Reports of self esteem and assertion were high (over 4 on a 1 to 5 point Likert scale) and also did not change significantly over time. These responses were consistent with prior studies of self-reported self esteem (see Baumeister et al., 2003, for a review).

Similar repeated measures ANCOVAs were conducted to determine whether the contextual factors changed over time (see Table 1). In 6th grades, young adolescents indicated that they perceived parental monitoring as occurring *most of the time* (again, over 4 on a 1 to 5 point Likert scale) but perceptions of monitoring decreased significantly over 6th, 7th, and 8th grades. In contrast, rates of delinquent friends increased significantly over this period. Young adolescents reported *some* engagement with violent media on average (over 3 on a 1 to 5 point Likert scale); engagement with violent media did not change significantly over time.

Correlations among constructs were also examined. Given the sample size, even correlations of small sizes were significant; therefore, correlations are discussed in terms of size. Associations among constructs were similar at each grade. As expected from prior studies (Coie & Dodge, 1998; Farrington, 2004), strong associations were found between delinquent behaviors and aggression (r = .72, r = .66, and r = .64 in 6th, 7th, and 8th grades, respectively). Grades in school, self esteem, and assertion were positively correlated but with Pearson correlation coefficients that were indicative of no meaningful association or a weak association even though the correlations were significant (*r*s ranging from .08 to .17). In addition, indicators of competence showed minimal to weak negative correlations with problem behaviors (*r*s ranging from –0.06 to –0.20). Although the correlations were significant, the size of the associations suggested that the two domains of functioning (i.e., competence and problem behaviors) were independent of each other in the middle school

Table 1. *Means and Standard Deviations for Key Variables*

	6th Grade		7th Grade		8th Grade			
Outcomes	**M**	**SD**	**M**	**SD**	**M**	**SD**	**Repeated Measures Effect**	η^2
Delinquency	3.36	4.98	5.61	6.85	6.47	7.85	$F(2, 2202) = 9.64$***	.01
Aggression	11.96	10.06	18.03	11.76	19.65	12.14	$F(2, 2198) = 28.68$***	.03
Grades	3.91	0.94	3.87	0.85	3.76	0.86	*ns*	
Self-esteem	4.20	0.76	4.12	0.81	4.10	0.84	*ns*	
Assertion	4.18	0.63	4.15	0.62	4.08	0.65	*ns*	
Contextual factors								
Friend delinquency	4.08	5.11	6.00	6.48	6.32	6.64	$F(2, 2174) = 7.47$**	.01
Parental monitoring	4.14	0.84	4.00	0.85	3.82	0.90	$F(2, 2054) = 10.28$***	.01
Violent media	3.17	.82	3.31	.80	3.27	.79	*ns*	

Note: Analyses controlled for race and ethnicity, school type, gender, and household structure; means adjusted for covariates were nearly identical to the unadjusted means shown in the table.
*$p < .05$. **$p < .01$. ***$p < .001$.

years. Associations among the contextual factors were in the weak to moderate range (*r*s ranging from –0.11 to 0.30) with significant, positive correlations between friend delinquency and engagement with violent media and significant, negative correlations for parental monitoring with the other two contextual factors.

Concurrent Regressions

Results from the concurrent regression at 6th grade are shown in Table 2. Regarding the two problem behaviors, all three contextual factors were significantly associated with rates of delinquency and aggression after accounting for the covariates in this study. Specifically, higher friend delinquency, higher engagement with violent media, and lower parental monitoring were associated with higher delinquency and aggression. Some of the covariates were also significantly associated with these outcomes. For both delinquency and aggression, gender was a significant covariate, with boys reporting higher rates than girls and African American or Black students having significantly higher rates than Latino or White students. Note that a more extensive analysis of gender differences in aggression and delinquency in this sample has been reported elsewhere (see Nichols, Graber, Brooks-Gunn, & Botvin, 2006). As can be seen in Table 2, covariates accounted for only a small percentage of the variance in problem behaviors whereas the contextual factors explained a more sizeable percentage of the variance in these behaviors ($\Delta R^2 = .39$ in both models).

For indicators of competence, effects of contextual factors were less pervasive and accounted for significant but small percentages of the variance in the constructs (see Table 2). A significant effect of engagement with violent media was found for grades in school, such that higher violent media engagement was associated with lower grades after accounting for the covariates (see Table 2), and a significant effect of parental monitoring was found for both self esteem and assertiveness such that more monitoring was associated with higher self esteem and more assertiveness after accounting for covariates. Some of the covariates were also associated with the indicators of competence. For example, boys were significantly more likely to have lower grades in school compared to girls, and students who were White were more likely to have higher grades in school than African American students. Attending public school was associated with higher levels of assertiveness. For self esteem, none of the covariates were significant.

Regressions Predicting Change Over Time

Hierarchical regressions were conducted to assess whether prior contextual factors predicted change in problem behaviors or indicators of competence over time, specifically from 6th to 7th grade, and from 7th to 8th grade. Results are shown in Tables 3 (6th to 7th grade) and 4 (7th to 8th grade). In all of these analyses, stability was seen for each outcome in that the same variable from the prior year significantly predicted the variable in the subsequent year and accounted for the largest percentage of variance in the models. In contrast with the concurrent model at 6th grade, contextual factors accounted for only a small percentage of the variance in the change in problem behaviors and competence over time.

For delinquency, parental monitoring and engagement with violent media significantly predicted change in delinquency from 6th to 7th grade and from 7th to 8th grade (see Tables 3 and 4). Specifically, lower parental

Table 2. *Hierarchical Regression Models Assessing Concurrent Associations at 6th Grade*

	Delinquency	Aggression	Grades	Self-Esteem	Assert
Step 1					
Gender	1.89 (0.30)***	1.68 (0.62)**	–0.18 (0.06)**	–0.04 (0.05)	0.02 (0.04)
Public	0.21 (0.38)	–0.25 (0.79)	–0.12 (0.07)	0.06 (0.06)	0.12 (0.05)*
Latino	–1.22 (0.36)**	–2.87 (0.74)***	–0.03 (0.07)	–0.08 (0.07)	0.03 (0.05)
White	–1.34 (0.46)**	–3.21 (0.95)**	0.49 (0.09)***	–0.14 (0.08)	–0.02 (0.06)
Other	–0.87 (0.51)	–1.30 (1.06)	0.15 (0.10)	0.01 (0.09)	0.09 (0.07)
Household	–0.26 (0.31)	–0.95 (0.65)	0.09 (0.06)	–0.09 (0.06)	–0.03 (0.04)
R^2	0.05***	0.03***	0.05***	0.01	0.01
Step 2					
Friend delinquency	0.51 (0.02)***	1.01 (0.05)***	–0.01 (0.01)	0.00 (0.01)	0.00 (0.00)
Monitoring	–0.92 (0.14)***	–1.44 (0.30)***	0.02 (0.04)	0.19 (0.03)***	0.09 (0.02)***
Violent media	0.59 (0.16)***	2.17 (0.32)***	–0.10 (0.04)**	–0.03 (0.04)	0.00 (0.03)
ΔR^2	0.39***	0.39***	0.01**	0.05***	0.02**
Final R^2	0.44	0.42	0.06	0.06	0.03
Final model *F*	*F*(9, 996) = 87.47***	*F*(9, 997) = 79.32***	*F*(9, 983) = 7.21***	*F*(9, 814) = 5.52***	*F*(9, 991) = 2.76**

Note. Unstandardized coefficients and standard errors are shown.
*$p < .05$. **$p < .01$. ***$p < .001$.

Table 3. *Hierarchical Regression Models Predicting Change From 6th to 7th Grade After Controlling for 6th Grade Outcomes and Covariates*

	Delinquency	Aggression	Grades	Self-Esteem	Assert
Step 1					
6th grade outcome	0.67 (0.04)***	0.58 (0.03)***	0.51 (0.03)***	0.40 (0.03)***	0.21 (0.03)***
R^2	0.22***	0.24***	0.30***	0.15***	0.05***
Step 2					
Gender	0.10 (.39)	−1.96 (0.65)**	−0.04 (0.05)	0.00 (0.05)	0.03 (0.04)
Public	0.75 (0.49)	0.64 (0.83)	−0.06 (0.06)	0.03 (0.06)	0.08 (0.05)
Latino	−0.35 (0.46)	−1.30 (0.79)	−0.05 (0.05)	−0.23 (0.06)***	0.01 (0.05)
White	−1.48 (0.59)*	−1.83 (1.00)	0.19 (0.07)**	−0.28 (0.08)***	−0.02 (0.06)
Other	−1.88 (0.66)**	−3.53 (1.12)**	−0.05 (0.08)	0.05 (0.09)	−0.01 (0.07)
Household	0.37 (0.40)	1.35 (0.68)*	−0.02 (0.05)	0.00 (0.05)	−0.06 (0.04)
ΔR^2	0.01*	0.02***	0.01	0.03***	0.01
Step 3					
Friend delinquency	0.11 (0.05)*	−0.07 (0.08)	−0.01 (0.01)	−0.01 (0.01)	0.00 (0.00)
Monitoring	−0.56 (0.24)*	−1.05 (0.40)**	0.02 (0.03)	0.06 (0.03)	0.09 (0.02)***
Violent media	1.45 (0.26)***	2.44 (0.44)***	−0.08 (0.03)**	−0.03 (0.04)	0.00 (0.03)
ΔR^2	0.04***	0.03***	0.01**	0.01*	0.01**
Final R^2	0.27	0.29	0.32	0.19	0.07
Final model F	F(10, 984) = 36.14***	F(10, 986) = 38.96***	F(10, 964) = 45.34***	F(10, 814) = 18.22***	F(10, 975) = 6.85***

Note. Unstandardized coefficients and standard errors are shown.
$*p < .05$. $**p < .01$. $***p < .001$.

monitoring and higher engagement with violent media were associated with higher rates of delinquent behaviors after accounting for prior delinquency and covariates. Delinquent friends only predicted change in delinquency from 6th to 7th grade such that more delinquent friends were associated with higher rates of delinquent behaviors after accounting for prior delinquency and covariates. The covariates demonstrated very little effect on change in delinquency over time. From 6th to 7th grade, African American to Black youth had greater increases than White or other youth, but race was not associated with changes in delinquency from 7th to 8th grades. Also, being male was associated with increased delinquency from 7th to 8th grade only.

For aggression, engagement with violent media and parental monitoring significantly predicted change in

Table 4. *Hierarchical Regression Models Predicting Change From 7th to 8th Grade After Controlling for 7th Grade Outcomes and Covariates*

	Delinquency	Aggression	Grades	Self-Esteem	Assert
Step 1					
7th grade outcome	0.68 (0.03)***	0.59 (0.03)***	0.58 (0.03)***	0.38 (0.03)***	0.31 (0.03)***
R^2	0.34***	0.32***	0.33***	0.13***	0.08***
Step 2					
Gender	0.86 (0.38)*	0.35 (0.60)	−0.12 (0.04)**	−0.04 (0.05)	−0.02 (0.04)
Public	0.45 (0.50)	0.26 (0.79)	−0.23 (0.06)***	0.06 (0.06)	−0.04 (0.05)
Latino	−0.58 (0.46)	−0.51 (0.72)	−0.11 (0.05)*	−0.10 (0.06)	−0.01 (0.05)
White	0.01 (0.59)	0.29 (0.93)	0.03 (0.07)	−0.13 (0.07)	−0.07 (0.06)
Other	0.51 (0.66)	−0.81 (1.04)	0.00 (0.07)	−0.28 (0.08)**	−0.10 (0.07)
Household	−0.48 (0.40)	−1.07 (0.63)	0.10 (0.04)*	0.04 (0.05)	−0.02 (0.04)
ΔR^2	0.00	0.00	0.02***	0.01*	0.00
Step 3					
Friend delinquency	0.02 (0.04)	−0.01 (0.06)	0.01 (0.00)	0.00 (0.00)	−0.01 (0.00)**
Monitoring	−0.73 (0.24)**	−0.70 (0.38)	0.05 (0.03)*	0.08 (0.03)**	0.07 (0.02)**
Violent media	0.98 (0.26)***	0.83 (0.42)*	−0.06 (0.03)*	−0.03 (0.03)	0.01 (0.03)
ΔR^2	0.02***	0.01	0.01*	0.01*	0.02***
Final R^2	0.36	0.33	0.36	0.15	0.11
Final model F	F(10, 1126) = 62.07***	F(10, 1125) = 54.38***	F(10, 1113) = 60.98***	F(10, 1132) = 19.70***	F(10, 1103) = 12.94***

Note. Unstandardized coefficients and standard errors are shown.
$*p < .05$. $**p < .01$. $***p < .001$.

aggression from 6th to 7th grades such that higher engagement with violent media and lower parental monitoring were associated with higher rates of aggression after accounting for prior aggression and covariates (see Table 3). Although the regression coefficient for engagement with violent media was significant in the model predicting change in aggression from 7th to 8th grades, this step was not associated with a significant change in R^2 (see Table 4). Friend delinquency was not associated with changes in aggression over time. In the model assessing change in aggression from 6th to 7th grade, girls had higher rates of change in aggression (i.e., increases) over time (consistent with Nichols et al., 2006), as did students from two parent households. Students in the other ethnic or racial group had lower rates of change in aggression overtime in comparison to African American students. No covariates significantly predicted change in aggression from 7th to 8th grade (see Table 4).

Predictors of change in the indicators of competence were also examined; however, as indicated, while mean scores on these variables decreased over time, overall change over time was not significant (see Table 1). For grades in school, engagement with violent media significantly predicted changes in school achievement from 6th to 7th grade and from 7th to 8th after accounting for covariates; in both analyses, higher engagement with violent media was associated with decreases in grades in school. Parental monitoring predicted changes in school achievement from 7th to 8th grade such that lower monitoring predicted declining scores. In analyses of change from 6th to 7th grade, White youth showed significantly less decline in grades in comparison to African American or Black youth. From 7th to 8th grades, boys demonstrated greater declines in grades, as did public versus parochial school students, and Latinos in comparison to African American or Blacks. Students from two parent households showed fewer declines in grades.

For self esteem, after accounting for initial levels of self esteem and covariates, only parental monitoring predicted change in self esteem from 7th to 8th grade such that lower parental monitoring was associated with lower self esteem over time. Being African American or Black was associated with less decrease of self esteem in comparison to other students in both analyses (see Tables 3 and 4 for specific associations).

Finally, for assertiveness, parental monitoring was a significant predictor of change in assertive behaviors from 6th to 7th grade and from 7th to 8th grade. In both analyses, higher reports of parental monitoring were associated with higher assertiveness after accounting for prior assertiveness and covariates. Furthermore, in the model assessing change from 7th to 8th grade, friend delinquency was also a significant predictor such that lower friend delinquency was associated with more assertiveness. None of the covariates were significant predictors of change in assertiveness over time.

Discussion

In general, each of the contextual factors we investigated was associated with concurrent aggression and delinquency in 6th grade as well as changes in aggression and delinquency over time. The only exception was that friend delinquency was not associated with increases in aggression over time. Findings for delinquency and aggression are in line with prior research which indicates that these behaviors develop from multidetermined pathways (e.g., Coie & Dodge, 1998; Moffitt et al., 2001). In contrast, contextual factors had less pervasive effects on indicators of competence. However, parental monitoring was salient to both self esteem and assertiveness and in protecting against declines in these areas over time (with the exception of change in self esteem from 6th to 7th grades). Also, engagement with violent media predicted decreases in school achievement over time along with an initial association with lower achievement at 6th grade. Thus, results indicate that family factors were salient across both risky and competent domains of functioning during the early adolescent period. Also, engagement with violent media contributed to unhealthy trajectories over time in terms of increases in aggression and delinquency, and decreases in academic achievement.

In this investigation, only one construct from each of the contextual domains was examined as the goal of the study was to examine factors associated with competence versus problem behaviors across domains rather than intensively within a domain. Future studies would benefit from the investigation of multiple indicators of a context to identify the most salient constructs within each domain (see other articles this volume). At the same time, we selected contextual factors that have commonly been linked to problem behaviors and have been included in prevention programming (e.g., Botvin & Griffin, 2004).

In particular, findings for parental monitoring are consistent with prior studies that have demonstrated protective effects of monitoring on problem behaviors (e.g., Fletcher, Steinberg, & Williams-Wheeler, 2004; Griffin et al., 2000). At the same time, this study is one of the only studies to demonstrate that monitoring was also protective against declines in self esteem and maintaining assertive behaviors. Other studies have reported positive links between quality of family relationships such as warmth or conflict on child outcomes (e.g., see Coie & Dodge, 1998; Cummings et al., 2000, for reviews) but in this investigation we focused specifically on the practice of monitoring adolescent activities. Importantly, this measure tapped the adolescent's perception that parents knew where he or she was or with whom the adolescent spent time. Of course, monitoring may be associated with parent–adolescent relationship quality in that adolescents who think their parents know about their activities may also have better relationships with their parents. Notably, parental monitoring has been considered a central component of prevention initiatives aimed at parents of young adolescents (e.g., Dishion & McMahon, 1998). Our findings demonstrate that monitoring not only offsets the development of risk but also promotes the development of competence.

In addition, we found evidence that more engagement with violent media was linked with problem behaviors in 6th grade and increases in these behaviors over time, as well as lower school achievement and decreases in achievement over time. These findings were not surprising given literature on exposure to violent media (Roberts et al., 2004). However, much of the prior literature has focused mainly on the effects of television violence and in recent years playing violent video games. In this investigation, it should be noted that our measure of violent media use was not lengthy or detailed in comparison to time use diary methods or more extended surveys. Rather, the measure assessed engagement with violent media across different forms of media—television, movies, music, and video games. Thus, youth who are immersing themselves in multiple types of violent media may be particularly at risk for poorer developmental outcomes during the middle school years.

However, we can not rule out the possibility that the deleterious effects of violent media engagement on academic achievement were not attributable to media use in general. That is, more time spent engaged with any type of media may result in less time spent on school work. It is important to keep in mind that engagement with violent media also predicted delinquency and aggression concurrently in 6th grade and over time, findings which would not necessarily be explained by engagement with any type of media. Future studies should examine this issue more closely potentially incorporating not only general media use and violent media use, but also possible positive media use, such as involvement in creation of media. In addition, much like studies of the effects of friend delinquency, it has been reported that youth who are already more aggressive may be more likely to engage in violent media use (Brown & Cantor, 2000; Roberts et al., 2004). Our study did not address this particular issue as our focus was on understanding the impact of multiple contextual factors on both problem behavior and competence. More detailed investigation of moderating effects (e.g., prior aggression levels) should be undertaken in future work on the role of media violence.

Although we replicated the negative effect of friend delinquency on aggression and delinquency, we found little evidence that this factor impacted competence. The only exception was that higher reports of friend delinquency were associated with lower assertiveness from 7th to 8th grades. As indicated, prevention programs targeting substance use and violence, such as the Life Skills Training Program (Botvin & Griffin, 2004) specifically teach assertiveness skills in order to offset initiation of problem behaviors during the middle school years. Yet, findings to date have been mixed with some studies reporting that higher assertiveness (when assessed in social interactions) was linked with higher rates of problem behaviors rather than lower rates (e.g., Wills et al., 1989). In our investigation, assertiveness as an indicator of competence was supported given that higher assertiveness was predicted by higher parental monitoring and lower friend delinquency suggesting that assertiveness resulted from positive predictors.

This investigation has some limitations. We examined problem behaviors and competence in a sample of urban, minority youth. Although it has often been suggested that it is important to examine the development of competence, in particular, rather than deficit models in studies of minority youth (Garcia Coll & Garrido, 2000), these findings may not generalize to other populations. In addition, our analyses were limited to those youth who continued to participate in the study over time. Our attrition analyses indicated that attrition was linked to more problems and greater contextual risk (e.g., higher rates of violent media use, delinquency, etc.). These biases would make it less likely that we would find effects for most constructs but interpretation of findings should be made in light of the longitudinal sample bias. Our study was also impacted by the assessment strategy employed. Specifically, all constructs were based on adolescent self report. Steps were taken to improve reporting of problem behaviors and rates of these behaviors were in line with national survey data (Nichols et al., 2006). However, it should be emphasized that contextual influences (e.g., parental or friend behaviors) reflect adolescent *perceptions* rather than independent report. In terms of the analyses and results, many effects were small. Given our sample size, we had ample power to detect small effects; small R^2 values were significant as were small changes in R^2. Although we have found several significant effects, clearly, other factors are salient to the constructs we have examined.

As we have suggested, this investigation was also limited by only examining one contextual factor for each domain. As such, examination of risks and protective factors within each domain were not included. That is, parental monitoring was a protective factor and promoted competence but a family related risk factor was not examined; whereas friend delinquency and engagement with violent media were risk factors and comparable positive or possibly protective factors from peer and media domains were not examined.

Finally, it is of note that indicators of competence and problem behaviors demonstrated little association in correlational analyses. Specifically, aggression and delinquency showed no meaningful association with grades in school, self esteem, or assertion suggesting that the examination of these constructs separately was warranted. However, person-centered analyses might have identified clusters of youth who were high in both, low in both, or who exhibited a combination of competent and problem behaviors.

As indicated, the goal of this investigation was to identify contextual factors that would not only predict engagement in problem behaviors, but also be linked to competence. Under the rubric of developmental psychopathology, factors that offset risk and promote competence would potentially have a strong payoff as components of prevention or health promotion programs. As such, our findings indicate that family factors, specifically increasing parental monitoring, as a target of intervention, would not only offset risk trajectories but enhance positive development. In addition, lowering engagement with violent media may offset risk and also be likely to enhance competence at least in the school domain. Continued application of developmental psychopathology frameworks are clearly merited given the needs of youth not only to avoid risk but to develop the skills and talents needed to meet the challenges of adolescence and adulthood.

References

Achenbach, T. M., & Edelbrock, C. S. (1986). *Teacher's report form.* Burlington: University of Vermont.

Baumeister, R. F., Campbell, J. D., Krueger, J. I., & Vohs, K. D. (2003). Does high self-esteem cause better performance, interpersonal success, happiness, or healthier lifestyles? *Psychological Science in the Public Interest, 4,* 1–44.

Botvin, G. J., & Griffin, K. W. (2004). Life Skills Training: Empirical findings and future directions. *Journal of Primary Prevention, 25,* 211–232.

Botvin, G. J., Schinke, S. P., Epstein, J. E., & Diaz, T. (1994). The effectiveness of culturally focused and generic skills training approaches to alcohol and drug abuse prevention among minority youth. *Psychology of Addictive Behaviors, 8,* 116–127.

Brown, J. D., & Cantor, J. (2000). An agenda for research on youth and the media. *Journal of Adolescent Health, 27S,* 2–7.

Catalano, R. F., Hawkins, J. D., Berglund, M. L., Pollard, J. A., & Arthur, M. W. (2002). Prevention science and positive youth development: Competitive or cooperative frameworks? *Journal of Adolescent Health, 31*(Suppl. 6), 230–239.

Catalano, R. F., Hawkins, J. D., Krenz, C., & Gillmore, M. (1993). Using research to guide culturally appropriate drug abuse prevention. *Journal of Consulting & Clinical Psychology, 6,* 804–811.

Cicchetti, D., & Cohen, D. J. (1995). Perspectives on developmental psychopathology. In D. Cicchetti & D. J. Cohen (Eds.), *Developmental psychopathology: Vol. 1. Theory and methods* (pp. 3–20). New York: Wiley.

Coie, J. D., & Dodge, K. A. (1998). Aggression and antisocial behavior. In W. Damon (Ed.) N. Eisenberg (Vol. Ed.), *Handbook of child psychology, Vol. 3. Social, emotional, and personality development* (5th ed., pp. 779–862). New York: Wiley.

Cummings, E. M., Davies, P. T., & Campbell, S. B. (2000). *Developmental psychopathology and family process.* New York: The Guilford Press.

Dishion, T. J., & McMahon, R. J. (1998). Parental monitoring and the prevention of child and adolescent problem behavior: A conceptual and empirical formulation. *Clinical Child and Family Psychology Review, 1,* 61–75.

Elliot, D., Huizinga, D., & Menard, S. (1989). *Multiple problem youth: Delinquency, substance use, and mental health problems.* New York: Springer-Verlag.

Englander-Golden, P., Elconin, J., & Satir, V. (1986). Assertive/leveling communication and empathy in adolescent drug abuse prevention. *Journal of Primary Prevention, 6,* 231–243.

Evans, R. I., Hansen, W. B., & Mittlemark, M. B. (1977). Increasing the validity of self-reports of smoking behavior in children. *Journal of Applied Psychology, 62,* 521–523.

Farrington, D. P. (2004). Conduct disorder, aggression, and delinquency. In R. M. Lerner & L. Steinberg (Eds.), *Handbook of adolescent psychology* (2nd ed., pp. 627–664). New York: Wiley.

Fletcher, A. C., Steinberg, L., & Williams-Wheeler, M. (2004). Parental influences on adolescent problem behavior: Revisiting Stattin and Kerr. *Child Development, 75,* 781–796.

Galassi, M. D., & Galassi, J. P. (1978). Assertion: A critical review. *Psychotherapy: Theory, Research, and Practice, 15, 16–29.*

Gambrill, E. D., & Richey, C. A. (1975). An assertion inventory for use in assessment and research. *Behavior Therapy, 6,* 550–561.

Garcia Coll, C., & Garrido, M. (2000). Minorities in the United States: Sociocultural context for mental health and developmental psychopathology. In A. J. Sameroff, M. Lewis, & S. M. Miller (Eds.), *Handbook of developmental psychopathology* (2nd ed., pp. 177–195). New York: Plenum.

Griffin, K. W., Botvin, G. J., Scheier, L. M., Diaz, T., & Miller, N. (2000). Parenting practices as predictors of substance use, delinquency, and aggression among urban minority youth: Moderating effects of family structure and gender. *Psychology of Addictive Behaviors, 14,* 174–184.

Harter, S. (1999). *The construction of the self.* New York: Guilford.

Ianni, F. A. J., & Orr, M. T. (1996). Dropping out. In J. A. Graber, J. Brooks-Gunn, & A. C. Petersen (Eds.), *Transitions through adolescence: Interpersonal domains and context* (pp. 285–321). Mahwah, NJ: Lawrence Erlbaum Associates, Inc.

Masten, A. S., Coatsworth, D. J., Neemann, J., Gest, S. D., Tellegen, A., & Garmezy, N. (1995). The structure and coherence of competence from childhood through adolescence. *Child Development, 66,* 1635–1659.

Masten, A. S., & Curtis, W. J. (2000). Integrating competence and psychopathology: Pathways toward a comprehensive science of adaptation in development. *Development and Psychopathology, 12,* 529–550.

Moffitt, T. E. (1993). Adolescence-limited and life-course persistent antisocial behavior: A developmental taxonomy. *Psychological Review, 100,* 674–701.

Moffitt, T. E., Caspi, A., Rutter, M., & Silva, P. A. (2001). *Sex differences in antisocial behavior: Conduct disorder, delinquency, and violence in the Dunedin longitudinal study.* Cambridge, England: Cambridge University Press.

Nichols, T. R., Graber, J. A., Brooks-Gunn, J., & Botvin, G. J. (2006). Sex differences in overt aggression and delinquency among urban minority middle school students. *Journal of Applied Developmental Psychology, 27,* 78–91.

Pajer, K. A. (1998). What happens to "bad" girls? A review of the adult outcomes of antisocial adolescent girls. *The American Journal of Psychiatry, 155,* 862–870.

Roberts, D. F., Henriksen, L., & Foehr, U. G. (2004). Adolescents and the media. In R. M. Lerner & L. Steinberg (Eds.), *Hand-*

book of adolescent psychology (pp. 487–521). New York: Wiley.

Rosenberg, M. (1965). *Society and the adolescent self-image*. Princeton, NJ: Princeton University Press.

Simmons, R. G., & Blyth, D. A. (1987). *Moving into adolescence: The impact of pubertal change and school context*. New York: Aldine.

Snyder H. N. (2003). *Juvenile Arrests 2001. Juvenile Justice Bulletin.* Washington, DC: Office of Juvenile Justice and Delinquency Programs, U.S. Department of Justice.

Tourangeau, R., Smith, T. W., & Rasinski, K. A. (1997). Motivation to report sensitive behaviors on surveys: Evidence from a bogus pipeline experiment. *Journal of Applied Social Psychology, 27,* 209–222

Wills, T. A., Baker, E., & Botvin, G. J. (1989). Dimensions of assertiveness: Differential relationships to substance use in early adolescence. *Journal of Consulting & Clinical Psychology, 57,* 473–478.

Received September 15, 2005
Final revision received October 19, 2005
Acepted October 20, 2005

Applied Developmental Science
2006, Vol. 10, No. 2, 86–95

Youths' Caretaking of Their Adolescent Sisters' Children: Its Costs and Benefits for Youths' Development

Patricia L. East
University of California, San Diego

Thomas S. Weisner
University of California, Los Angeles

Barbara T. Reyes
University of California, San Diego

This study examined how time spent caring for a teenage sister's child and experiences in providing care related to youths' young adult outcomes. Latino and African American youths (N = 108) were studied during middle and late adolescence. Results indicated that youths who provided many hours of child care were more stressed and had lower school grades but also reported a greater life satisfaction, a stronger school orientation, and were less likely to drop out of school. Negative experiences in providing care were associated with a lower likelihood of school dropout and teenage pregnancy. Findings suggest that the extent of sibling caregiving in teenage child-bearing families incurs both developmental costs and benefits.

In families with a teenage childbearing daughter, where the teenager and her baby live with the teen's family of origin after the baby is born, all available family members are typically pooled to help care for the adolescent's child. Child care provided by the teenager's younger siblings is a common and adaptive practice (Burton, 1995), yet how this caretaking impacts youths within these households is virtually unknown. Like most cooperative family system practices, there are likely to be both costs and benefits to any one family member. There are concerns, for example, that sibling caregivers miss out on their own developmentally appropriate experiences, are taking on adult responsibilities too soon, and that they will have diminished schooling and career aspirations (Dodson & Dickert, 2004; Lareau, 2003). Studies also show that children's extensive kin care obligations, including high levels of sibling care, can bear psychological and educational costs, such as experiencing stress, frequent school absences, problems in school, and school dropout (Brown-Lyons, Robertson, & Layzer, 2001; Fine & Zane, 1991). Conversely, much research from anthropological and developmental studies of children's care of their younger siblings shows that such care promotes children's empathy, perspective-taking, and social understanding (Bryant, 1989; Howe & Ross, 1990; Zukow, 1989). Sibling caregiving also provides an important context for building self-sufficiency and maturity and for teaching children to balance their self-concerns with the needs of others (Weisner, 1982, 2001; Zukow-Goldring, 1995).

The apparent inconsistencies with regard to the developmental impact of sibling caregiving may be clarified by considering the socioeconomic and cultural conditions under which care is provided. Sibling care within teenage childbearing families, for example, is often a necessary social and economic adaptation to the unique conditions such families face (Burton, 1990). Because such families are typically poor and have limited monetary resources for day care, sibling care provides a necessary and convenient economic function. With the teenage parenting sister needing to stay in school and work in order to receive governmental aid, and with the parents in the household working in order to provide the family income, younger sibling child care may be the only option that many of these families have. As such, sibling care is an essential component of a dynamic and cooperative system of care and is likely to be obligatory (Burton & Stack, 1993).

It is widely recognized that sibling caretaking socializes and prepares youth for parenting (Weisner, 1987; Zukow-Goldring, 1995). It has also been suggested that, within teenage parenting families, youths' socialization for parenthood occurs early in life by way of caring for an older sister's child (Burton, 1995). In

This research was supported by Grants R01-HD043221 from the National Institute of Child Health and Human Development, and APR-000970 from the Office of Population Affairs. We thank Leanne Jacobson for supervising the collection of data for this study.

Correspondence should be sent to Patricia L. East, the University of California, San Diego, Department of Pediatrics, 9500 Gilman Drive, Mail Code 0927, La Jolla, CA 92093-0927. E-mail: peast@ucsd.edu

thinking about younger siblings' outcomes, then, it is possible that youths' child care experience could instill a sense of parenting competence and lead them to minimize the hardships involved in early parenting. Such perceived child care competence may give rise to less diligence in pregnancy prevention and pave the way toward an early pregnancy among the younger siblings themselves (East, 1998). It is also plausible, however, that extensive time in child care leads younger siblings to fully realize the demands involved in raising a child of one's own and thwarts a desire for early parenting. This study examined the association between youths' hours of child care and their subsequent likelihood of a teenage pregnancy.

Youths' child care obligations also likely compete with their available time for school work and time with friends. Indeed, particularly for minority adolescents in working-class families, family obligations constitute a significant distraction from the time youth are able to spend on homework, in school activities, or on their own leisure, extracurricular activities (Fuligni, 2001; Larson & Verma, 1999). Given the results of several studies that show that children's extensive household labor and family care work deride youths' academic motivation (Dodson & Dickert, 2004; Fine & Zane, 1991; Gager, Cooney, & Call, 1999), we expected that youth who engage in large amounts of child care to disengage from school. Such school disengagement can take the form of low achievement aspirations, poor school grades, and, ultimately, school dropout.

Youths' experiences in child care and their willingness to provide care are also important in assessing its impacts. Is care provided willingly and spontaneously, or begrudgingly and resentfully? Positive experiences would support the prosocial and altruistic role of youth cooperating and helping their family in ways in which they are able (Bryant, 1992). However, resentful care (siblings arguing about it, feeling mad about it) may indicate coercion on the part of family members and foreshadow developmental costs (Dodson & Dickert, 2004). Indeed, others have also noted that adolescents report feeling exploited or harassed when asked to help with household or family work, and show evidence of stress and fatigue when family demands become overly burdensome (Larson & Verma, 1999). Certainly, the experiences youth have in various contexts can affect their development by promoting opportunities for skill building and identity consolidation, or for promoting stress and maladaptation (Theokas & Lerner, this issue). This was our intent here, to determine not only how much time youth engage in care within their family context but also to examine their experiences in the context of child care and its ramifications for development.

All families involved in this study were either Latino (Mexican American) or African American. Cooperative kin-based child care strategies are typically stronger in African American and Latino families relative to Anglo American families (Burton, 1996; Uttal, 1999), and sibling care is more common and is a more significant family obligation among Latino and African American adolescents than among White adolescents (Fuligni & Pederson, 2002). In Latino and Black families, then, sibling care may be an accepted and expected response to a teen's child's care. However, many current-day Mexican American families are "divided between borders," with some key family members living in Mexico and some family members living in the United States (Buriel & DeMent, 1997). Having key child care providers residing in Mexico would likely boost the levels of sibling care within Latino families relative to African American families, where kin are generally in closer proximity and more able to care for relatives (Burton & Stack, 1993). In this study, we examine the levels of sibling care by race/ethnicity and whether many hours of caretaking is more likely to be associated with unfavorable outcomes for Latinos or for African Americans.

This Study

This study examined youths' involvement in the caretaking of their teenage sister's child and how these experiences were associated with their adjustment as young adults. A previous article using the data presented in this report showed that girls who provided many hours of child care during middle adolescence (12 hr or more a week) reported pessimistic school aspirations, positive intentions to have a child right away, and permissive sexual behavior (East & Jacobson, 2001). In this study, we ask how the extent of child care provided during middle adolescence is related to youths' outcomes as evidenced during young adulthood. Study outcomes were felt stress, life satisfaction, school grades, school orientation, school dropout, and teenage pregnancy. Some of the study participants had experienced a teenage pregnancy themselves or had dropped out of school at follow up. Were these the individuals who provided more or less child care at middle adolescence? We also attempted to uncover the extent to which youths' positive and negative experiences in providing care were related to their young adult functioning. Such experiences may be more meaningful than the amount of time spent in child care. Finally, we examined whether high levels of child care were more likely to be associated with unfavorable outcomes for Latinos or African Americans and for girls or for boys. Girls may value and desire greater participation in child care than boys based on gender role expectations and socialization (Kroska, 2003). Thus, high levels of child care involvement may not be as detrimental for girls' outcomes as for boys.

Method

Participants

Participants were part of a longitudinal research study investigating the developmental trajectories of the younger siblings of childbearing teens (East & Jacobson, 2001). The study involved 146 early adolescents (55% girls) who were coresiding with an older teenage childbearing sister. Sixty-four percent of participants identified themselves as Latino (Mexican American), and 36% self-identified as African American. Almost all youth were from low-income or working-class families, and all lived in or around San Diego, California.

Youth were recruited into the study by first identifying eligible older sisters. Primigravida 15- to 19-year-old women were recruited during their pregnancy or immediately postpartum from a university hospital Teen Obstetric Clinic (35%), four nearby Planned Parenthood Clinics (24%), and by snowball sampling (41%). Research staff screened patients in clinic waiting rooms prior to their prenatal or postpartum appointments. If the teen and her family qualified for the study, they were asked to participate. Ninety percent of all eligible families invited to participate did so.

Families were eligible for the study if (a) there was an 11- to 15-year-old younger sibling and a primigravida 15- to 19-year-old older sister; (b) they were either Latino or African American; (c) both the younger sibling and the older sister were currently living together with their (biological) mother, and they had lived together for at least the last five years; and (d) no other child within the family (or within the household) had become pregnant or fathered a child as a teen. Thus, in all families, only one teenager was either currently pregnant for the first time or parenting her first child.

The data presented in this report were gathered at a first and second follow-up of the initial intake. (The primary variable of interest—i.e., siblings' time in child care—was not assessed at intake.) Follow-up 1 was conducted 1.5 years after the initial intake, and Follow-up 2 occurred 3.3 years after Follow-up 1. Of the 146 younger siblings of pregnant and parenting teens who participated at intake, 140 were relocated at Follow-up 1 and reinterviewed (or 96%). Of these, 135 were still living with their teenage sister and her child and provided information on the number of hours of child care. At Follow-up 2, 118 youth were relocated and reinterviewed (or 84% of those who participated at Follow-up 1). Of these, 108 younger siblings were found to be still living with their older sister and her child. These 108 younger siblings comprise the primary participants for this study.

Younger sibling participants were an average age of 13.6 years at intake (*SD* = 1.9), 15.1 years at Follow-up 1, and 18.5 years at Follow-up 2. Youth who participated at Follow-up 2 did not differ significantly in background characteristics (e.g., race/ethnicity, age, family income, mothers' educational level, etc.) from youth who did not participate at Follow-up 2. Sixty three percent of the 108 participating youth were Latino (*n* = 68), and 37% were African American (*n* = 40).

Fifty three percent of study families were receiving some form of governmental aid at Follow-up 1 (e.g., food stamps; Medi-Cal; or Women, Infants and Children services), and 37% were receiving some form of aid at Follow-up 2. About two thirds of teenage parenting sisters were receiving Temporary Assistance for Needy Families (TANF) at Follow-up 1, and slightly less than half were receiving TANF at Follow-up 2. Follow-ups 1 and 2 were conducted after 1996 (subsequent to welfare reform) and, thus, teenage parenting sisters needed to participate in high school or equivalent training and live at home in order to receive cash aid. At both study time points, approximately 40% of older (parenting) sisters and half of youths' mothers were working outside the home. The average total annual family income was approximately $14,000 for an average family of five.

The older sisters' children were, on average, 15 months old at Follow-up 1 (age range: 6 months to 19 months) and 4.6 years at Follow-up 2 (*SD* = 1.5). Fifty-three percent of teenagers' children were boys. Older sisters were an average age of 17.6 years at delivery (*SD* = 1.4), 19.8 years at Follow-up 1, and 23.2 years at Follow-up 2 (*SD* = 1.6).

Procedure

At each assessment, two female research assistants (who were fluent in Spanish) visited the younger siblings at their homes where they completed a short face-to-face interview and a self-administered questionnaire. The home visits lasted about 1 hr. All participants were paid $10 at each assessment and all were assured of the confidentiality and anonymity of their responses.

Measures

The study questionnaire contained 192 questions at Follow-up 1 and 271 questions at Follow-up 2, with several skip patterns so that most participants did not complete all questions.

The questionnaires at both times of assessment had an approximate 4th-grade reading level (as ascertained by the Flesch-Kincaid readability method). Scale scores were formed by averaging all of the items unless otherwise noted. All indicators of youths' young adult outcomes were drawn from Follow-up 2. The mean scores and standard deviations of all scale scores are shown in Table 1.

Extent of child care. The number of hours per week that youth cared for their teenage sister's children was asked by interview at both follow-ups. After the appropriate sister and child had been identified, the interviewer asked younger sibling participants, "How many hours a week do you take care of or look after your teenage sister's child (even in the presence of others)?"

Experiences in providing care. Youths' experiences in providing child care were operationalized in terms of positive experiences and negative experiences. Positive experiences were assessed by averaging youths' responses to the two items "I learn a lot about parenting by caring for my niece or nephew" and "I learn a lot about children by caring for my niece or nephew." Negative experiences were assessed by four items that asked how often the youth argued with his or her sister about having to provide care, felt mad about having to provide child care, felt that providing care interfered with the things they wanted to do, and did not like providing care. Response options ranged from 1 to 5, with high scores of positive experiences indicating learning a lot (Cronbach $\alpha = .87$), and high scores of negative experiences indicating frequent arguing, interfering, and feeling mad about (Cronbach $\alpha = .71$). These items were included on the study questionnaire at Follow-up 2 only.

Felt stress. Youths responded to eight questionnaire items drawn from the Perceived Stress Scale that asked, for example, how often within the last 3 months they felt stressed, anxious, burned out, or exhausted (Cohen, Kamarck, & Mermelstein, 1983). Response options ranged from 1 (*not at all*) to 5 (*a lot*). The Cronbach alpha of the eight items was .89.

Life satisfaction. Youths responded to four items on the questionnaire that asked how satisfied, proud, disappointed (reversed), and happy they were with the way things had turned out for them (based on the Satisfaction with Life Scale; Diener, Emmons, Larsen, & Griffin, 1985). Response options ranged from 1 to 5, such that high scores reflect a high life satisfaction. The Cronbach alpha of the four items was .76.

School grades. Youths were asked to indicate the grades they usually got in school, such that 8 = *mostly* As, 7 = *about half* As *and half* Bs, 6 = *mostly* Bs, 5 = *about half* Bs *and half* Cs, and so on. The possible score range was 1 to 8.

School orientation. Youths responded to four questions on the questionnaire that asked about the importance that he or she graduate from high school, get good grades in school, go to college, and get a good job, and to four questions about the likelihood that he or she would graduate from high school, go to college, get a good job, and how many years of education he or she would probably attain—for example, 1 (*not finish high school*) to 5 (*go to graduate school or a professional school after college*). Response options ranged from 1 (*not very important* or *not very likely*) to 5 (*very important* or *very likely*), wherein high scores reflect a high importance and likelihood placed on school and career

Table 1. *Mean Scores of Study Variables*

	M	*SD*	Range	*n*	%
Youths' age at FU1	15.1	1.9	13 to 17		
Youths' gender[a]	—	—	—		
Girls				59	55
Boys				49	45
Youths' race/ethnicity[b]	—	—	—		
Latino				68	63
African American				40	37
Youths' hours of care at FU1	10.6	13.4	0 to 85		
Youths' hours of care at FU2	14.0	23.5	0 to 168		
Negative experiences in care at FU2	2.3	1.1	1 to 5		
Positive experiences in care at FU2	4.1	1.1	1 to 5		
Felt stress at FU2	2.9	1.0	1 to 5		
Life satisfaction at FU2	3.4	1.0	1 to 5		
Grades at FU2	5.0	1.4	1 to 8		
School orientation at FU2	3.8	0.9	1 to 5		
School dropout by FU2[c]	—	—	—	33	31
Teen pregnancy by FU2[c]	—	—	—	41	38

Note: FU1 = Follow-up 1; FU2 = Follow-up 2.
[a]Coded as 0 = *boy*, 1 = *girl*. [b]Coded as 0 = *African American*, 1 = *Latino*. [c]Coded as 0 = *no*, 1 = yes.

achievements. Using this sample, the internal reliability (Cronbach alpha) of these eight items was .83.

School dropout. Youth were asked on the interview whether they had ever dropped out of school for any period of time. This item was scored as 0 = *never dropped out* and 1 = *had dropped out.*

Teen pregnancy. Youths responded on the questionnaire whether they had ever been pregnant (for girls) or gotten someone pregnant (for boys) before their 19th birthday. Response options were 0 = *no* and 1 = *yes.*

Results

Analytic Plan

The first level of analysis involved intercorrelating all study variables to determine how, on a pairwise basis, youths' background characteristics (age, gender, race/ethnicity), youths' hours of care, youths' experiences in care, and youths' adjustment were interrelated. We next examined how youths' hours of care and their experiences in care were related to their young adult outcomes. To address this, we computed multiple regression analyses on the outcomes of felt stress, life satisfaction, school grades, school orientation, school dropout and teenage pregnancy. Logistic regressions were computed for the latter two variables given that these were coded dichotomously. Predictor variables in the regressions were youths' hours of care at Follow-up 1 and Follow-up 2, their negative and positive experiences in providing care (at Follow-up 2), and the interaction between hours of care and their positive experiences, and the interaction between hours of care and their negative experiences. The results of the interactions will indicate whether outcomes are uniquely related to many hours of care and frequent negative experiences or to many hours of care and frequent positive experiences independent of either condition alone. Participants' age, race/ethnicity, and gender were entered as controls in these equations. Finally, to determine whether many hours of care are more likely to be associated with unfavorable outcomes for girls or for boys and for Latinos or African Americans, we computed regressions and included the interaction terms between number of hours of care and gender and number of hours of care and race/ethnicity. Experiences in providing care were not included in these regression equations.

Descriptive Statistics

The mean scores and standard deviations of all scale scores are shown in Table 1. These scores indicate that youths provided, on average, 11 hr of child care per week during middle adolescence and 14 hr of child care per week during late adolescence. There was large variability in the hours of care at both times of assessment, or between 0 and 85 hr per week at Follow-up 1, and between 0 and 168 hr per week at Follow-up 2. Most youths reported learning a lot about children and parenting by providing care (e.g., 77% responded "yes, sort of true," or "yes, really true" to both items), and most youths reported no negative experiences in providing care (e.g., 66% never or rarely argued about providing care, and 80% never or hardly ever felt mad about having to provide care). Of the 108 youths analyzed in this study, 33 indicated at Follow-up 2 that they had at one time dropped out of school (31%), and 28 girls and 13 boys reported that they had experienced (or caused) a teenage pregnancy (38%).

Interrelations Among Study Variables

Results of the correlational analysis (shown in Table 2) indicated that, at both assessment points, girls were more likely than boys to provide child care for their sisters' children. Latino youth were more likely than African American youth to provide care during middle adolescence (only). Younger aged youths were more likely to report both negative and positive experiences in providing care than older aged youths, and girls were more likely than boys to report negative experiences in negotiating care. The correlational results also showed that, although the number of hours youth spent providing care (at Follow-up 1 or Follow-up 2) was not significantly related to their adjustment outcomes during young adulthood, youths' reports of negative experiences in providing care were associated with a strong school orientation and a reduced likelihood of school dropout. Youths' positive experiences in providing care were associated with a high life satisfaction and a reduced likelihood of teenage pregnancy.

Child Care Hours and Experiences as Predictors of Young Adult Outcomes

Results of the multiple regressions (shown in Table 3) indicated that hours of child care provided at Follow-up 1 were positively related to a greater life satisfaction and a lower likelihood of school dropout at Follow-up 2. Hours of child care provided at Follow-up 2 were positively related to more felt stress, lower school grades, and a stronger school orientation at Follow-up 2. Youths' reports of negative experiences in providing care were related to a more positive school orientation and a significantly reduced likelihood of both school dropout and teenage pregnancy. Youths' reports of positive experiences in providing care were also associated with a reduced likelihood of a teenage pregnancy. There was a significant interaction between hours of

Table 2. *Intercorrelations Among Study Variables*

	1	2	3	4	5	6	7	8	9	10	11	12	13
1. Youths' age FU1	—												
2. Youths' gender[a]	-.00	—											
3. Youths' race/ethnicity[b]	.02	.01	—										
4. Youths' hours of care FU1	-.05	.26**	.21*	—									
5. Youths' hours of care FU2	-.12	.36***	-.01	.10	—								
6. Negative experiences in care FU2	-.25*	.29**	.15	.18	.11	—							
7. Positive experiences in care FU2	-.21*	-.18	.10	.03	.09	-.05	—						
8. Felt stress FU2	.26**	.28**	-.09	.08	.14	.17	-.04	—					
9. Life satisfaction FU2	-.33**	-.33***	-.08	.17	-.03	-.06	.21*	-.32**	—				
10. Grades FU2	-.15	.16	.03	-.09	.02	.07	-.01	-.07	.20	—			
11. School orientation FU2	-.15	.04	-.23*	.02	-.02	.20*	-.07	.17	.24*	.11	—		
12. School dropout by FU2	.42***	.10	.10	-.15	.03	-.27*	-.16	-.02	-.51***	-.25*	-.33***	—	
13. Teen pregnancy by FU2	.43***	.22*	.14	-.04	-.01	-.16	-.26**	.01	-.31**	-.13	-.24*	.35***	—

Note: $N = 108$ youths. FU1 = Follow-up 1; FU2 = Follow-up 2.
[a]Coded as 0 = *boy*, 1 = *girl*. [b]Coded as 0 = *African American*, 1 = *Latino*.
$^{*}p < .05$. $^{**}p < .01$. $^{***}p < .001$.

Table 3. *Regression Estimates of Youths' Hours and Experiences in Child Care on Their Young Adult Outcomes*

	Felt Stress		Life Satisfaction		Grades		School Orientation	
	β	*t*	β	*t*	β	*t*	β	*t*
Age	.22	2.14*	–.27	2.74**	–.08	—	–.16	—
Gender[a]	.11	—	–.39	3.43**	.31	2.31*	–.13	—
Race/ethnicity[b]	–.13	—	–.18	—	.06	—	–.31	3.09**
Hours of child care at FU1	.02	—	.34	3.47**	–.16	—	.11	—
Hours of child care at FU2	.39	2.22*	.06	—	–.42	2.14*	.35	2.04*
Negative experiences at FU2	.18	—	–.07	—	–.01	—	.21	2.00*
Positive experiences at FU2	.01	—	.10	—	.05	—	–.11	—
Negative Experiences × Hours of Child Care at FU2	–.17	—	.05	—	.15	—	–.25	1.98*
Positive Experiences × Hours of Child Care at FU2	–.26	1.99*	–.10	—	.34	2.25*	–.31	2.28*
$F(df = 9, 99)$	2.37*		4.02***		1.20		2.61**	
Adjusted R^2	.11		.21		.03		.13	

	School Dropout[c]			Teen Pregnancy[c]		
	Parameter Estimate	Odds Ratio	95% CI	Parameter Estimate	Odds Ratio	95% CI
Age	.57**	1.76	1.2 to 2.5	.49**	1.64	1.2 to 2.2
Gender[a]	–.77*	0.46	0.2 to 1.0	–.55	0.58	0.3 to 1.0
Race/ethnicity[b]	–.45	0.64	0.4 to 1.2	–.30	0.74	0.4 to 1.2
Hours of child care at FU1	–.30*	0.93	0.9 to 1.0	–.01	0.99	1.0 to 1.0
Hours of child care at FU2	–.08	0.93	0.7 to 1.2	.00	1.00	1.0 to 1.0
Negative experiences at FU2	–.46*	0.23	0.1 to 0.8	–.60*	0.55	0.3 to 1.0
Positive experiences at FU2	–.13	0.88	0.4 to 1.9	–.49*	0.61	0.4 to 1.0
Negative Experiences × Hours of Child Care at FU2	.05	1.05	1.0 to 1.1	–.03	0.97	0.9 to 1.0
Positive Experiences × Hours of Child Care at FU2	–.05	1.00	0.9 to 1.0	.00	1.04	1.0 to 1.1
–2LL ($df = 9$) =	30.88***			30.22***		
McFadden's rho squared	0.273			0.231		

Note: N = 108 youths. FU1 = Follow-Up 1; FU2 = Follow-Up 2; CI = confidence interval; LL = likelihood-ratio statistic.
[a]Coded as 0 = *boy*, 1 = *girl*. [b]Coded as 0 = *African American*, 1 = *Latino*. [c] Coded as 0 = *not experienced*, 1 = *experienced*.
*$p < .05$. **$p < .01$. ***$p < .001$.

care and negative experiences in care for youths' school orientation (β = –.25). Post-hoc analyses revealed that youths had the highest school orientation scores when they provided few hours of child care but reported many negative experiences in providing that care. There was also a significant interaction between hours of care and positive experiences in care for felt stress (β = –.26), school grades (β = .34) and school orientation (β = –.31). Post-hoc analyses showed that youths experienced the highest levels of stress and had the lowest grades when providing many hours of care and reporting few positive experiences in providing care. Youths also had the lowest school orientation scores when providing many hours of child care and reporting many positive experiences in providing that care.

Interactions Between Hours of Care and Gender and Race/Ethnicity

To determine whether many hours of care might be more strongly associated with negative outcomes for girls as opposed to boys, we computed regressions similar to those described above except using the predictors of age, gender, race/ethnicity, hours of care at Follow-up 1, hours of care at Follow-up 2, and the two interaction terms of hours of care at Follow-up 1 × Gender, and hours of care at Follow-up 2 × Gender. Results showed a significant interaction between hours of care at Follow-up 2 × Gender for the outcome of school dropout (β = –.13, odds ratio = .88, $p < .05$; not shown in a table). Post-hoc analyses comparing boys and girls with high and low hours of care indicated that, for those who provided many hours of care during young adulthood (or more than 10 hr per week), girls were significantly more likely to drop out of school than were boys. The respective dropout rates were 43% for girls and 14% for boys.

To determine whether many hours of care might be more strongly associated with negative outcomes for Latinos as opposed to African Americans, we computed regressions as described above except using the two interaction terms of hours of care at Follow-up 1 × Race/Ethnicity and hours of care at Follow-up 2 × Race/Ethnicity. Results of these analyses indicated a significant interaction between hours of care at Follow-up 1 × Race/Ethnicity for the outcome of teenage pregnancy ($\beta = .07$, odds ratio = 1.70, $p < .01$). Results of post-hoc analyses comparing Latinos and African Americans with high and low hours of care indicated that, for African American youth only, providing many hours of care during middle adolescence (8 or more hours per week) was associated with a significantly greater likelihood of experiencing a teenage pregnancy as opposed to providing few hours of care. The respective teenage pregnancy rates were 57% for those in the high care group and 24% for those in the low care group.

Discussion

The results of this study begin to reveal how youths' involvement in and experiences with caring for their adolescent sister's child are associated with their young adult functioning. We suggested earlier that sibling care, like most complex family practices, is neither an unequivocally positive nor negative experience, and that both favorable and unfavorable outcomes might ensue. Such a mixed pattern was indeed found. Results indicated that youths who provided many hours of child care were more stressed and had lower school grades, but also were happier, more optimistic about their futures, and more likely to stay in school (not drop out). Extensive involvement in the care of a teenage sister's child, then, may incur some benefits while also compromising, to some extent, youths' mental health and academic performance. It may be that extensive child care involvement deromanticizes parenting and reinforces a commitment to educational goals and school completion. Thus, contrary to other studies that have found that extensive involvement in sibling care is associated with school problems (Dodson & Dickert, 2004; Fine & Zane, 1991), these results suggest that high levels of child care may motivate youth to do well in school and to stay in school. The apparent contradictory findings of high levels of child care being associated with both low grades and a strong school orientation highlights the independence of these constructs, with school grades an objective indicator of one's academic performance, whereas school orientation (as assessed here) reflecting one's achievement motivation, values and goals (Eccles & Wigfield, 2002). Thus, although many hours of child care may impede youths' school performance, it appears to strengthen their drive to succeed.

It is interesting that the two unfavorable outcomes (high stress, low school grades) were associated with the extent of care as provided during late adolescence, suggesting that excessive time in child care may have more negative ramifications when performed later in adolescence as opposed to earlier. This may also reflect the cumulative impact of providing much care over several years. In addition, the older sisters were also older at Follow-up 2, and younger siblings may increasingly resent spending many hours caring for the children of their now adult older sisters. This resentment may take the form of high stress and burn out.

Youths' experiences in providing care were also important for their functioning as young adults. Indications of coerced care (arguing with sister, feeling mad about it) were related to several favorable outcomes, such as a positive school orientation, a lower likelihood of school dropout, and a reduced likelihood of teenage pregnancy. This suggests that youths who are striving to do well in school, to graduate, and to avoid pregnancy are most aggravated by their obligations of kin care. In this case, coercive kin care obligations may be interfering with youths' own life goals and "collude to keep particular individuals wedded to family needs" (Burton & Stack, 1993, p. 163). These results also speak to the importance of both the context within which care is provided and youths' feelings about providing care. Others have also noted that children's feelings about their work contributions to the family are more important for children's development than the actual work itself (Goodnow & Lawrence, 2001).

This study's results also indicated that positive experiences gained through providing child care—or beliefs that one was learning a lot about parenting and children—were associated with a reduced likelihood of teenage pregnancy. This may reflect the increased appreciation of all that is involved in parenting a young child and serve to reinforce delayed childbearing among younger siblings. This is a critical finding that highlights the valuable lessons that can be learned through the realistic and long-term experiences of caring for an infant or small child on a daily basis. Such practical lessons are part of many pregnancy prevention programs aimed at youth and could be highly beneficial.

To our knowledge, this study is among the first to examine the child care provided by the younger siblings of teenage mothers. As a first step in a relatively new area, this study was admittedly exploratory and had several limitations. One limitation was that it utilized self-report recall of hours of care. Youth may over- or underestimate their level of care (Dodson & Dickert, 2004), and retrospective reports may be inaccurate. Observational assessments of the care actually provided or random time sampling (Larson, 1989) would have helped verify self-reports. In addition, outcomes related to youths' maturity, empathy, and prosocial behaviors were not assessed in this study and, thus, child care impacts on these outcomes could not be addressed (Weisner, 2001).

It is also important to note that the question used to identify siblings' extent of childcare included the wording "*take care of or look after your teenage sister's child* (*even in the presence of others*"). We do not know, then, if older sisters or youths' mothers were absent, present, or remaining in the vicinity to oversee. This precluded a differentiation of independent sibling care versus sibling care as an ancillary back-up and the importance of this distinction for youths' young adult adjustment (Burton, 1995). This study also lacked information on the child care provided by key family members, including the teen mother herself, youths' parents (the baby's grandparents), and the baby's father (the teen's partner). The roles of these individuals likely affect overall care resources and their omission precluded a full understanding of the diversity and complexity of kin caregiving patterns within teenage childbearing families.

In addition, had we been able to do qualitative and ethnographic work with these families, or with a nested subset of them, we would have been able to speak more directly about the processes occurring within these blended kin care systems in which younger siblings participate. There are clearly strong and ongoing negotiations occurring among the teen mother, her siblings, and other household kin as they work together to raise the teen's baby. How this care is negotiated and what the sibling caretakers' roles are within this system are important questions emerging from this study that would require a "closer-in, experience-near" study of these processes (Weisner, 1982, 1996).

This sample also focused only on younger siblings who lived continuously with their teenage sister and her children across a 3-year period. Families in which sibling care is shorter lived or less continuous (in cases where the teen, her child, or the sibling move out of the household) may offer another view of sibling care that was not provided in this study. Too, the eligibility criteria specified that all families were comprised of a mother, a teenage older sister, and an (eligible aged) younger sibling. This necessitated that other family constellations (mother-absent families, families in which a grandparent or other relative is the primary parental figure) were excluded. Although such restrictive eligibility criteria limit the generalizeability of findings, we believe the current results are relevant to the families represented here or those families in which parenting teenagers remain with their family of origin. Recent national data indicate that close to 80% of teenagers continue to reside with their family of origin one year after they give birth and that most teen mothers live in households with one or more siblings (Manlove, Mariner, & Papillo, 2000).

This sample is also of young infant and toddler-age children being cared for by their teenage mothers and her family. It is currently unknown what the impacts of this pattern of care are for the teen's child, not to mention the young mother herself. Having shown the salience and rather high frequency of sibling care within teenage childbearing families, impacts on the teen mother and her child would be an important area for further study.

Despite these limitations, however, this study's findings highlight that siblings are an integral component of a dynamic and cooperative shared caregiving system within families that have teenage childbearing daughters. Sibling caregiving is clearly an important part of the family system's adaptation to the unique demands of early parenting. On a broader scope, these findings also illustrate the developmental costs and growth opportunities associated with a single social experience, that of providing family care (Youngblade & Curry, this issue). Indeed, others have also noted the apparently contradictory outcomes and experiences associated with adolescents' kin care and kin work (Brown-Lyons et al., 2001). A full understanding of the opportunities for positive change associated with kin caregiving requires a more complete understanding of the various experiences gained in this context (Theokas & Lerner, this issue), and of the complex ways in which caregiving roles are negotiated and maintained over time. Siblings as caregivers offer many potential benefits for promoting positive youth development, such as learning kindness, cooperation, and concern for others. Future youth development programs could incorporate such opportunities for promoting positive change.

References

Brown-Lyons, M., Robertson, A., & Layzer, J. (2001). *Kith and kin – informal child care: Highlights from recent research.* New York: Columbia University National Center for Children in Poverty.

Bryant, B. K. (1989). The child's perspective of sibling caretaking and its relevance to understanding social-emotional functioning and development. In P. Zukow (Ed.), *Sibling interactions across cultures: Theoretical and methodological issues* (pp. 245–270). New York: Springer-Verlag.

Bryant, B. K. (1992). Sibling caretaking: Providing emotional support during middle childhood. In F. Boer & J. Dunn (Eds.), *Children's sibling relationships: Developmental and clinical issues* (pp. 55–69). Hillsdale, NJ: Lawrence Erlbaum Associates, Inc.

Buriel, R., & DeMent, T. (1997). Immigration and sociocultural changes in Mexican, Chinese, and Vietnamese American families. In A. Booth, A. Crouter, & N. Landale (Eds.), *Immigration and the family: Research and policy on U.S. immigrants* (pp. 165–200). Mahwah, NJ: Lawrence Erlbaum Associates, Inc.

Burton, L. M. (1990). Teenage childbearing as an alternative life-course strategy in multigeneration Black families. *Human Nature, 1,* 123–143.

Burton, L. M. (1995). Intergenerational patterns of providing care in African-American families with teenage childbearers: Emergent patterns in an ethnographic study. In V. L. Bengtson, K. W. Schaie, & L. M. Burton (Eds.), *Adult intergenerational relations: Effects of societal change* (pp. 79–96). New York: Springer.

Burton, L. M. (1996). Age norms, the timing of family role transitions, and intergenerational caregiving among aging African American women. *The Gerontologist, 36,* 199–208.

Burton, L. M., & Stack, C. B. (1993). Conscripting kin: Reflections on family, generation, and culture. In A. Lawson & D. L. Rhode (Eds.), *The politics of pregnancy: Adolescent sexuality and public policy* (pp. 174–185). New Haven, CT: Yale University Press.

Cohen, S., Kamarck, T., & Mermelstein, R. (1983). A global measure of perceived stress. *Journal of Health and Social Behavior, 24,* 385–396.

Diener, E., Emmons, R. A., Larsen, R. J., & Griffin, S. (1985). The Satisfaction with Life Scale. *Journal of Personality Assessment, 49,* 71–75.

Dodson, L., & Dickert, J. (2004). Girls' family labor in low-income households: A decade of qualitative research. *Journal of Marriage and Family, 66,* 318–332.

East, P. L. (1998). Impact of adolescent childbearing on families and younger siblings: Effects that increase younger siblings' risk for early pregnancy. *Applied Developmental Science, 2,* 62–74.

East, P. L., & Jacobson, L. J. (2001). The younger siblings of teenage mothers: A follow-up of their pregnancy risk. *Developmental Psychology, 37,* 254–264.

Eccles, J. S., & Wigfield, A. (2002). Motivational beliefs, values, and goals. *Annual Review of Psychology, 53,* 109–132.

Fine, M., & Zane, N. (1991). Bein' wrapped too tight: When low-income women drop out of high school. *Women's Studies Quarterly, 1 & 2,* 77–99.

Fuligni, A. J., (2001). Family obligation and the academic motivation of adolescents from Asian, Latin American, and European backgrounds. In A. J. Fuligni (Ed.) *Family obligation and assistance during adolescence* (pp. 61–76). New York: Jossey-Bass.

Fuligni, A. J., & Pederson, S. (2002). Family obligation and the transition to young adulthood. *Developmental Psychology, 38,* 856–868.

Gager, C. T., Cooney, T. M., & Call, K. T. (1999). The effects of family characteristics and time use on teenagers' household labor. *Journal of Marriage and the Family, 61,* 982–994.

Goodnow, J. J., & Lawrence, J. A. (2001). Work contributions to the family: Developing a conceptual and research framework. In A. J. Fuligni (Ed.), *Family obligation and assistance during adolescence* (pp. 5–22). New York: Jossey-Bass.

Howe, N., & Ross, H. S. (1990). Socialization, perspective-taking, and the sibling relationship. *Developmental Psychology, 26,* 160–165.

Kroska, A. (2003). Investigating gender differences in the meaning of household chores and child care. *Journal of Marriage and Family, 65,* 456–473.

Lareau, A. (2003). *Unequal childhoods: Class, race, and family life.* Berkeley: University of California Press.

Larson, R. W. (1989). Beeping children and adolescents: A method for studying time use and daily experience. *Journal of Youth and Adolescence, 18,* 511–530.

Larson, R. W., & Verma, S. (1999). How children and adolescents spend time across the world: Work, play, and developmental opportunities. *Psychological Bulletin, 125,* 701–736.

Manlove, J., Mariner, C., & Papillo, A. R. (2000). Subsequent fertility among teen mothers: Longitudinal analyses of recent national data. *Journal of Marriage and Family, 62,* 430–448.

Uttal, L. (1999). Using kin for child care: Embedment in the socioeconomic networks of extended families. *Journal of Marriage and the Family, 61,* 845–857.

Weisner, T. S. (1982). Sibling interdependence and child caretaking: A cross-cultural view. In M. Lamb & B. Sutton-Smith (Eds.), *Sibling relationships: Their nature and significance* (pp. 305–327). Hillsdale, NJ: Lawrence Erlbaum Associates, Inc.

Weisner, T. S. (1987). Socialization for parenthood in sibling caretaking societies. In J. B. Lancaster, J. Altman, A. Rossi, & L. Sherrod (Eds.), *Parenting across the life span* (pp. 237–270). New York: Aldine de Gruyter.

Weisner, T. S. (1996). Why ethnography should be the most important method in the study of human development. In R. Jessor, A. Colby, & R. Shweder (Eds.), *Ethnography and human development: Context and meaning in social inquiry* (pp. 305–324). Chicago: University of Chicago Press.

Weisner, T. S. (2001). Children investing in their families: The importance of child obligation in successful development. In A. J. Fuligni (Ed.), *Family obligation and assistance during adolescence* (pp. 77–83). New York: Jossey-Bass.

Zukow, P. G. (Ed.) (1989). *Sibling interactions across cultures: Theoretical and methodological issues.* New York: Springer-Verlag.

Zukow-Goldring, P. (1995). Sibling caregiving. In M. H. Bornstein (Ed.), *Handbook of parenting* (Vol. 3, pp. 177–208). Mahwah, NJ: Lawrence Erlbaum Associates, Inc.

Received September 15, 2005
Final revision received October 5, 2005
Accepted October 18, 2005

Applied Developmental Science
2006, Vol. 10, No. 2, 96–106

The People They Know: Links Between Interpersonal Contexts and Adolescent Risky and Health-Promoting Behavior

Lise M. Youngblade and Laura A. Curry
University of Florida

This study examined (a) relations between multiple interpersonal contexts and sustained risky and health-promoting behavior over a 2-year period and (b) health care outcomes of this behavior. Two hundred and ninety 13- to 19-year olds completed 2 phone surveys assessing negative and positive behavior and risk and protective factors in multiple interpersonal contexts. Across context, constructs related to resources, interpersonal connection, and control emerged to predict positive and negative behavior. Adolescents engaging in sustained risky behavior used more health care and had higher expenditures than those who were not; youth engaging in sustained health-promoting behavior had fewer encounters with the health care system and were less costly than those who were not. Findings are discussed relevant to current research on adolescent behavior and policy for intervention and prevention.

A number of comprehensive theoretical models of adolescent risky and problem behavior propose risk and protective factors at multiple levels (Catalano & Hawkins, 1996; Jessor, 1998; Lerner & Simi, 2000; Moffit, Caspi, & Rutter, 2001; Resnick et al., 1997). At the same time, growing attention is focused on promoting positive youth development, encouraging health-promoting behavior, and investing in resources for youth (Benson, Leffert, Scales, & Blyth, 1998; Hawkins, Catalano, & Miller, 1992; Lerner & Simi, 2000).

Central to these models is a focus on contexts of social relationships. In fact, multiple developmental theories (e.g., attachment, social learning, relationship, and ecological–transactional theories) emphasize the importance of relationships and relationship context to understanding social development (Bandura, 1977; Bowlby, 1982; Cicchetti & Aber, 1998; Hinde & Stevenson-Hinde, 1987; Sroufe, 1997). Moreover, research demonstrates the relevance of social relationships for adolescents in negotiating new developmental tasks and transitions (Schulenberg, Maggs, & Hurrelmann, 1997; Silbereisen, 1998), and recent reviews document the importance of multiple proximal and distal relationship contexts in the development of risk behaviors and youth development more generally (e.g., Ferrer-Wreder, Stattin, Lorente, Tubman, & Adamson, 2004; Petraitis, Flay, & Miller, 1995).

This research was supported by a Grant (R03 HS013261) to Lise Youngblade, Ph.D., from the Agency for Healthcare Research and Quality, US Department of Health and Human Services.

Correspondence should be sent to Lise M. Youngblade, Ph.D., Institute for Child Health Policy, University of Florida, 1329 SW 16th Street, Room 5130, Gainesville, FL 32608. E-mail: lmy@ichp.ufl.edu

Significant empirical work reveals important links between specific interpersonal contexts and various types of risky and health-promoting behavior. For example, studies have illuminated peer processes and their association with the onset and escalation of risky behavior such as substance abuse and delinquency (Dishion, Capaldi, Spracklen & Li, 1995; Dishion, McCord, & Poulin, 1999) as well as with risk preference and risky decision making (Gardner & Steinberg, 2005). Other research, for example, examines the connections between sibling relationships and teen pregnancy (East & Jacobson, 2000). In addition, multiple aspects of parenting have been related to both risky and healthy behavior (Biglan et al., 1996; Gorman-Smith, Tolan, & Henry, 1999; Griffin, Botvin, Sheier, Diaz, & Miller, 2000). Connections to health-promoting behavior, that is, behavior that ensures current and future physical and mental health, are less well articulated, even though researchers point out that adolescence is a critical time for establishing health-related habits that will persist into adulthood (Heubner, 2003; Maggs, Schulenberg, & Hurrelmann, 1997). Factors that have been identified include having parents who model healthy behaviors (Jessor, Turbin, & Costa, 1998) and having high levels of parent–family connectedness and school connectedness (Resnick et al., 1997).

More distally, community-based research demonstrates the importance of interpersonal aspects of communities in decreasing risky behavior and providing greater opportunities for positive youth development. Community investments in "social capital" and resources for youth (e.g., activities for youth, adults as role models) are related to lower levels of risky behavior in the community and greater opportunity for health-promoting behavior and positive youth development (Benson et al., 1998; Heubner, 2003; Youngblade, Curry, Novak, Vogel, & Shenkman, 2006). In addition, congruent with social control theory, which posits that weak "bonds" to societal institutions free the adolescent from the prescriptive norms that discourage risk-taking behavior (Hirschi, 1969), communities that utilize effective and appropriate mechanisms of control and where members feel "connected" to one another, provide contexts that both discourage problem behavior and encourage positive and competent youth behavior (Hawkins et al., 1992; Roth & Brooks-Gunn, 2000).

Although much has been learned from these efforts, several critical issues still remain. First, much of this research focuses on single risky or health-promoting behaviors, and single relationship contexts (see also Steinberg & Avenevoli, 1998). Although there are notable exceptions such as the National Longitudinal Study of Adolescent Health (e.g., Klein, 1997; Resnick et al., 1997; Udry & Bearman, 1998), the Seattle Social Development and Communities that Care Projects (e.g., Catalano & Hawkins, 1996; Hawkins et al., 1992; Mrazek, Biglan, & Hawkins, 2004), and the 4-H Study of Positive Youth Development (Lerner et al., 2005; Theokas & Lerner, this issue), comprehensive studies that simultaneously examine the predictive power of multiple domains, and include both risk and protective factors are few. Moreover, while recent discussions include the importance of not only reducing risky behavior but also increasing health-promoting behavior, studies that simultaneously include both dimensions of adolescent health-related behavior are limited, especially when considered from a multilevel contextual framework. This is unfortunate given the fact that many risky (and healthy) behaviors may co-occur, and that adolescents interact with people across multiple contexts.

Thus, in this study, we build on this literature by assessing the simultaneous impact of various aspects of multiple interpersonal contexts (i.e., family, peer, school, community) on both risky and health-promoting behavior. In general, these contextual aspects are based on "social capital" tenets (Edelman, Bresnen, Newell, Scarbrough, & Swan, 2004; Tsai & Ghoshal, 1998) and concepts from the literature on community building to promote positive youth development (Benson et al., 1998; Hawkins et al., 1992; Jessor, 1998). These dimensions include structural (i.e., provision of resources and activities), relational (quality of relationships, such as warmth and trust), and cognitive (shared visions or paradigms to promote collective goals, such as control) characteristics.

Second, it bears noting that numerous and varied behaviors are defined as "risky behavior," including illegal drug use, gambling, tobacco and alcohol use, delinquency, inappropriate aggressiveness and violence, school failure, and unsafe sexual activity. However, many studies focus on only one type of risky behavior, even though many adolescents participate in more than one type of risk behavior, and the combined effect of participation in multiple behaviors is concerning (Dryfoos, 1990; Lerner & Simi, 2000; Youngblade, Col, & Shenkman, 2002). Thus, in keeping with problem behavior theory and other theoretical approaches emphasizing the co-occurrence of problem behaviors (Jessor, 1998; Moffitt et al., 2001), for this study we adopted an inclusive definition of risky behavior as participation in any of a broad spectrum of risk behaviors. The development of an empirical and theoretical rubric for defining health-promoting behavior is much less advanced in the literature, so for the purposes of this study, we followed the same logic we applied to defining risky behavior, and utilized a composite index of health-promoting behavior.

Third, related to the issue of defining risky behavior is the issue of behavioral pattern. Prior empirical research highlights adolescents at greatest risk as those who engage in sustained risky behavior over a period of time, as opposed to those who engage in episodic experimentation (e.g., Moffitt et al., 2001; Silbereisen, 1998). Thus, in this study we identified these "at-risk" youth and compared them to all others. On the positive side, following similar logic, we identified youth who were engaging in sustained health-promoting behavior over time and compared them to all others.

Thus, the first goal of this study was to examine the relations between aspects of interpersonal connection, control, and resource provision in multiple interpersonal contexts (family, peer, school, community) and the odds of engaging in both risky and health-promoting behavior. The outcome variables were composites of multiple behaviors, which were then dichotomized to identify adolescents displaying sustained risky (and, separately, health-promoting) behavior over a 2-year period of time versus others.

Matters of Policy

Although extant literature describes multilevel predictors of adolescent risky behavior, absent in large part are policy-related connections to health-care utilization and cost outcomes. This is unfortunate given the sentiment that simply understanding the reasons for adolescents' risky behaviors cannot be expected to improve the health status of adolescents (Irwin, Cataldo, Matheny, & Peterson, 1992; Klein, 1997). Merging the predictors of adolescents' risky behaviors with adolescents' actual health-care use and concomitant expenditures can, however, point the direction to targeting health-care and community resources into prevention and guidance programs for adolescents, particularly for adolescents at highest risk. For example, in a state-wide analysis of 28,000 adolescents enrolled in a public low-income health insurance program, we found that adolescents who engaged in risky behavior utilized significantly more healthcare services than those who did not, especially in high cost service settings like the emergency room (ER). In fact, when considered from a pool level, the 15% of the adolescents who engaged in risky behavior that resulted in a health-care consequence accounted for about 40% of the annual expenditures to care for the entire pool of adolescents (Youngblade et al., 2002). Moreover, subsequent multilevel modeling analyses of community level risk and protective factors (e.g., community risky behavior rates, violence, and social capital) showed that, after controlling for individual-level sociodemographic characteristics of the adolescent as well as other community-level indicators, community investment in social capital predicted lower levels of risky behavior, increased utilization of outpatient and preventive health-care, and lower overall health-care expenditures (Youngblade et al., 2006). Clearly, then, identifying contexts for risky behavior prevention and health promotion may not only portend positive developmental outcomes for adolescents, but also positive effects for the health care system. Thus, our second goal was to examine health care outcomes of sustained risky and health-promoting behavior.

Method

Data were collected as part of a larger, short-term longitudinal study of adolescent health (Curry & Youngblade, in press; Youngblade et al., 2006). Originally, adolescents were recruited from the Florida Healthy Kids Program, the largest component of Florida's Title XXI State Children's Health Insurance Program program. The Healthy Kids Program provides health care to children and adolescents (ages 5 to 19) in low-income families, whose income is between 100% and 200% of the Federal Poverty Level and who do not qualify for Medicaid. As part of the study, a comprehensive survey of health, risky and health-promoting behavior, healthcare access, community risks and resources, and interpersonal supports and challenges was conducted with 576 adolescents who were randomly selected from the program.

One year later, these 576 adolescents were contacted and asked to participate in a follow-up telephone survey that assessed the same dimensions. Two hundred and ninety adolescents participated at both Time1 and Time 2. Of the 286 remaining participants from Time 1, 190 adolescents were not reached due to changes in telephone numbers with no forwarding information, disconnected phones, phone numbers that were no longer valid for the target adolescent, and attempts that never resulted in contact with anyone at the number dialed. (Up to 27 attempts were made for each participant from Time 1.) In addition, 10 parents refused to give permission to have their son or daughter interviewed, and 86 adolescents declined.

A professional survey center at the University of Florida conducted all of the interviews for this study. Owing to the sensitive nature of some of the questions asked, all interviewers were women. A $15 WalMart giftcard was mailed to all participants after each survey.

Participants

Participants included 290 adolescents (173 girls, 59.66%) who were between the ages of 13 and 19 at Time 1 (M = 14.98, SD = 1.56). In terms of race and ethnicity, 77 (26.55%) were Hispanic, 44 (15.17%) were African American, 161 (55.52%) were non-Hispanic White, and 8 (2.76%) were of "Other" ethnic heritage. Of the respective households, 175 (60.34%) were two-parent families, and 115 (39.66 %) were single-parent or other-type families. Mean family size was 4.1 (SD = 1.36). Mean family income was $25,807 ($SD$ = 10,153).

Analyses of sample attrition revealed a slight bias in terms of age and gender. At Time 1, adolescents who participated at both time points (M = 14.98, SD = 1.56) were significantly younger than those who did not participate at Time 2 (M = 15.47, SD = 1.65), t (574) = 3.68, $p < .001$. In addition, a greater proportion of females (59.66%) participated at both time points than at Time 1 only (50.00%): χ^2 (1, N = 575) = 5.42; $p < .05$. There were no significant differences between groups in terms of reported risk behavior, health-promoting behavior, income, race, or ethnicity.

Outcome Measures

Risky behavior. Items used in the current survey to assess participation in risky behavior were modified from items included in the Youth Risk Behavior Surveillance System (Grunbaum et al., 2002), the Communities That Care® Youth Survey (Developmental Research and Programs, Inc., 1999), and the National Longitudinal Study of Adolescent Health (e.g., Resnick et al., 1997). In the current study, six categories of risk behavior were assessed with 22 specific items: tobacco use (1 item), alcohol use (2 items), illegal drug use (9 items), truancy and school suspension (2 items), sexual activity (2 items), and crime and violence (6 items).

Participants were asked first whether they had ever engaged in each activity, and second about the frequency of engagement over the previous 12 months. Responses were coded 0 (*never*) to 5 (*every or almost every day*). Items measuring behavioral frequency were summed to form a global risky behavior composite. This 22-item summary had a mean of 3.87 (SD = 6.18) at Time 1 and 6.25 (SD=8.67) at Time 2 and ranged from 0 (*no risk behavior ever*) to 102 (*multiple and frequent risk behavior*).

Approximately 70% of all participants reported engagement in at least one risk behavior, 60% reported two or more risk behaviors. These rates are similar to those reported by participants of nationally representative surveys, such as the Monitoring the Future Study (Johnston, O'Malley, & Bachman, 2001) and the Youth Risk Behavior Surveillance System (Grunbaum et al., 2003).

Self-reported health-promoting behavior. Two items were used to measure the extent to which adolescents engaged in health-promoting behavior: How often do you wear a seatbelt (0 = *never*, 4 = *all of the time*)? How often do you engage in physical activities either in or out of school (0 = *never*, 4 = *every or almost every day*)? Responses were summed at Time 1 (M = 4.62; SD = 2.50) and at Time 2 (M = 5.06; SD = 1.77). The majority of adolescents reported engaging in both, but varied in frequency.

Sustained behavior. To identify sustained high behavior over time, we created groups based on scores at Time 1 and Time 2. For both risky behavior and health-promoting behavior, distributions at both Time 1 and Time 2 were examined and split at the median. From these dichotomous scores at each time point (i.e., above or below median), summary variables were created that represented behavior above the median at both times versus all others: sustained risky behavior (1) versus all others (0); and sustained health-promoting behavior (1) versus all others (0). One hundred and six (36.55%) were identified as being above the median at both Time 1 and Time 2 in risky behavior; 61 (21.03%) were above the median in health-promoting behavior at both time points. There was little overlap between the two (χ^2 (1, N = 290) = 2.51, *ns*), and only 17 (6%) engaged in both sustained risky and protective behavior.

Predictor Variables

Sociodemographic characteristics. Adolescents were asked to report their age, in completed years. In addition, they reported on ethnicity (Black, White, Hispanic, Other; collapsed to White/non-Hispanic versus all others for the analyses), gender (female, male), and household status (two-parents at home versus "other" family situation). Metropolitan specification (metropolitan versus rural) was based on rural–urban commuting area (RUCA) codes applied to the adolescent's home zip code. RUCA codes use zip codes to delineate metropolitan and nonmetropolitan settlements based on the size and direction of primary commuting flows (Morrill, Cromartie, & Hart, 1999).

Measures of the family context. Measures of both the parent relationship and the sibling relationship were included in the family context. First, six variables were created to reflect various aspects of the parent–adolescent relationship. Four of these variables utilized Likert scales. Items on the first three of these four scales were rated on a 5-point Likert scale ranging from 1 (*strongly disagree*) to 5 (*strongly agree*). The fourth scale utilized a 5-point scale ranging from 1 (*not at all wrong*) to 5 (*very wrong*). In all four cases, items on each scale were summed to form a composite indicator.

Parental attachment (38 items, α = .92, M = 115.14, SD = 26.32) was measured with the parent subscale from the Inventory of Parent and Peer Attachment (Armsden & Greenberg, 1987). This scale included items such as "My parents trust my judgment" and "I tell my parents about my problems and troubles." Second, adolescents responded to 7 items about household rules (α = .70, M = 16.48, SD = 3.76; Communities That Care® Youth Survey; Developmental Research and Programs, Inc., 1999), including items like, "The rules in my family are clear" and "My parents ask if I've gotten my homework done." Third, parental supervision (5 items, α = .68, M = 8.56, SD = 1.72) was assessed via questions such as "How much does/do your parent(s) know who your friends are?" adapted from measures in the Families in Communities project (Coley & Chase-Lansdale, 2000). Finally, parents' tolerance for risky behavior (6 items, α = .73, M = 1.37, SD = 1.93; Communities That Care® Youth Survey, Developmental Research and Programs, Inc., 1999) was measured with items such as "How wrong do your parents feel it would be for you to smoke cigarettes?"

The final parent–adolescent relationship dimension that was assessed was parenting style (Steinberg, 1987). For this measure, adolescents were asked to indicate who made the following decisions about the adolescent's activities: "How late at night I can stay out"; "Who I hang out with"; "How I spend my money"; and "Where I can hang out." Response categories for these items were 1 (*parents decide*), 2 (*parents decide after we discuss*), 3 (*we decide together*), 4 (*I decide after we discuss*), and 5 (*I decide*). Three variables were created to measure parents' use of authoritarian, permissive, and authoritative parenting styles. The number of 5 responses was set to measure use of a permissive parenting style; the number of 1 responses was set to reflect the use of an authoritarian parenting style; and the number of 2, 3, and 4 responses indicated authoritative parenting styles. Because this is an ipsative measure, authoritarian and permissive styles were included in the model, and the referent category is authoritative. Means for the authoritarian and permissive parenting variables were .64 (SD = .80) and 1.53 (SD = 1.19), respectively.

To assess the extent of sibling negative influence, adolescents were asked whether siblings had ever engaged in each of the five following items: drank alcohol, smoked cigarettes, smoked marijuana, taken a handgun to school, been suspended or expelled from school (Communities That Care® Youth Survey, Developmental Research and Programs, Inc., 1999). *Yes* (1 = *yes*) responses were summed (M = 1.17, SD = 1.44).

Measures of the peer context. Four components of adolescent–peer relationships were assessed. First, the 25-item peer attachment scale from the Inventory of Parent and Peer Attachment (Armsden & Greenberg, 1987) was used. Items on this scale were rated on a 5-point Likert scale ranging from 1 (*strongly disagree*) to 5 (*strongly agree*). This scale includes items reflecting communication (e.g., "My friends encourage me to talk about my difficulties"), trust (e.g., "My friends accept me as I am"), and alienation (e.g., "I feel alone or apart when I am with my friends") that are summed to form a composite score (α = .92, M = 80.97, SD = 13.49).

In addition, positive peer influence (27 items, α = .92, M = 7.97, SD = 2.70) and negative peer influence (3 items, α = .78, M = 12.09, SD = 13.73) were measured with individual items such as "How many of your friends will go to college?" (valid responses were *all, most, about half, some,* and *none*) and "How many of your four best friends smoked cigarettes during the past 12 months?" (valid responses were 0 to 4). Responses were summed to create negative and positive influence composites, respectively. Items were adapted from the Iowa Youth and Families Project (Elder, & Conger, 2000), the Families in Communities Project (Coley & Chase-Lansdale, 2000) and the Communities That Care® Youth Survey (Developmental Research and Programs, Inc., 1999). Finally, adolescents were asked to indicate whether they typically spent unstructured social time "hanging out" with friends and with a boyfriend/girlfriend after school but before dinner (range = 0 to 2; M = 1.20, SD = 0.74; Communities That Care® Youth Survey, Developmental Research and Programs, Inc., 1999).

Measures of the school context. Three school-related measures were included in the survey. First, as a proxy for school connectedness, adolescents were asked to indicate the grades (M = 6.08, SD = 1.61) that they normally received on report cards, from 0 (*mostly* Fs) to 8 (*mostly* As). Participation in organized extracurricular school-related activities was assessed by having adolescents indicate whether they participated in 10 organized after-school activities on a typical day (M = 3.31, SD = 1.93). These 10 activities included sports team participation, cheerleading, drama club, and so on. Finally, adolescents were asked to indicate how many times they changed schools since kindergarten from 0 (*never*) to 4 (*7 or more times*; M = 2.07, SD = 1.00; item adapted from the Communities That Care® Youth Survey; Developmental Research and Programs, Inc., 1999).

Measures of the community context. Adolescents' perceptions of their community were assessed by two measures (Communities That Care® Youth Survey, Developmental Research and Programs, Inc., 1999). To assess the extent to which communities provided positive resources and opportunities for youth, adolescents were asked to indicate which of the following activities were available to young people in their communities: sports teams, scouting, boys and girls clubs, 4-H clubs, and volunteering opportunities. *Yes* responses (1 = *yes*) were summed (α = .74, M = 3.20, SD = 1.54). Second, adolescents' perceptions of community control was measured with eight items (8 items, α = .80, M = 14.53, SD = 6.40) such as "If you wanted to, how easy would it be for you to get some beer, wine, or hard liquor," and "If you wanted to, how easy would it be for you to get a handgun?" Responses were coded with a 4-point Likert scale ranging from 0 (*very easy*) to 3 (*very hard*).

Health-Care Use and Costs

Health-care use and costs were calculated from claims and encounter data files provided by the Florida Healthy Kids Program. These files contained International Classification of Diseases 9th Revision Clinical Modification codes, Physician's Current Procedural Terminology (CPT) codes, inpatient hospitalization codes, and dates of service.

A total monthly health care use rate was developed for each adolescent, that was the sum of all outpatient, inpatient, and ER use averaged across the 12-month period between surveys. Outpatient use rates were calculated from the number of unique days on which a CPT code appeared in the claims and encounter record, and included all preventive and acute care services in office, clinic, and hospital settings. ER and inpatient use rates were developed using the presence of an ER code or a hospital admission date in the records.

Because of their proprietary nature, health-care cost data were not available from the health plans that contract with the Florida Healthy Kids Program. Therefore, we utilized standardized fee data from two sources to estimate health-care costs. Accordingly, outpatient charges were calculated by applying a standardized national fee schedule (Practice Management Information Corporation, 1998) to outpatient claims (we conservatively used fees at the 50th percentile). Inpatient and ER charges were calculated using data from Florida's Hospital Cost Containment Board (HCCB). We applied the mean charges from the HCCB data to the adolescents' inpatient and ER claims. Monthly per capita total expenditures were calculated as the sum of inpatient, outpatient, and ER health-care expenditures and averaged across the 12-month period. Because of distributional skew, expenditures were log-transformed for analyses.

Results

Results are presented in two parts. In the first, multivariate relations between the contextual domains and sustained risky and health-promoting behavior are examined. In the second, analyses of heath-care outcomes are considered.

Contextual Predictors of Sustained Risky and Health-Promoting Behavior

A series of bivariate correlations were run between the demographic and contextual predictors and the behavioral outcomes. Of the demographic variables, only age and gender were significantly related to the outcomes, such that the likelihood of sustained risky behavior increased with age and boys had a higher likelihood of sustained health-promoting behavior than girls. With respect to the contextual domains, the majority of variables within each context were related in expected ways to the behavioral outcomes. Table 1 presents these correlations.

To examine the multivariate relations between the contextual predictors and the behavioral outcomes, logistic regressions were conducted separately for sustained risky and sustained health-promoting behavior. Each regression included demographic controls and the interpersonal–contextual variables representing families, peers, schools, and communities. Because we were interested in the concurrent analysis of multiple contexts, all variables were entered into the regression simultaneously. Table 2 presents the results of these regressions.

With respect to the demographic variables, age was significantly and positively associated with sustained risky behavior, and gender was the only significant demographic predictor of sustained health-promoting behavior. Older adolescents were significantly more likely to engage in sustained risky behavior than were younger adolescents. In the case of gender, girls were

Table 1. *Correlations Between Sustained Risky and Health-Promoting Behavior and Predictors*

Predictor Variable	Sustained Risky Behavior	Sustained Health-Promoting Behavior
Demographic controls		
Age	.39***	–.05
Gender[a]	.01	–.18**
Ethnicity[b]	–.06	–.01
Household status[c]	–.08	.05
Residence[d]	–.00	–.06
Family relationship context		
Parental attachment	–.29***	.16**
Authoritarian parenting	–.24***	.08
Permissive parenting	.26***	–.14*
Parental tolerance of risky behavior	.32***	–.14*
Household rules	–.35***	.13*
Parental supervision	–.34***	.07
Sibling negative influence	.35***	–.12*
Peer relationship context		
Peer attachment	–.10	.12*
Peer positive influence	–.21***	.21***
Peer negative influence	.55***	–.13*
Unstructured social time	.32***	.01
School context		
Grades	–.13*	.13*
Organized activities	–.13*	.27***
School instability	.12*	–.11
Community context		
Positive community resources	–.09	.14*
Community control	–.40***	.06

[a]1 = female, 0 = male. [b]1 = non–Hispanic White, 0 = all others. [c]1 = two–parent household, 0 = one–parent or other household. [d]1 = urban residence, 0 = rural residence.
*$p < .05$. **$p < .01$. ***$p < .001$.

Table 2. *Logistic Regression of Sustained Risky Behavior and Health–Promoting Behavior on Demographic and Context Variables*

	Sustained Risky Behavior			Sustained Health–Promoting Behavior		
	Parameter Estimate	***SE***	**Odds Ratio (Confidence Intervals)**	**Parameter Estimate**	***SE***	**Odds Ratio (Confidence Intervals)**
Demographic controls						
Age	.36**	.13	1.44 (1.13, 1.84)	.06	.13	0.94 (0.72, 1.22)
Gender[a]	–.03	.38	0.97 (0.46, 2.05)	–.86***	.42	0.16 (0.07, 0.36)
Ethnicity[b]	.16	.36	1.17(0.58, 2.38)	–.27	.37	0.76 (0.37, 1.56)
Household status[c]	–.44	.38	0.64 (0.30, 1.34)	.18	.39	1.20 (0.56, 2.57)
Metropolitan residence[d]	.56	.51	1.75 (0.64, 4.80)	–.51	.49	0.60 (0.23, 1.58)
Family context						
Parent attachment	–.01	.01	0.99 (0.97, 1.01)	.33*	.23	1.38 (1.08, 2.18)
Authoritarian parenting	–.58**	.23	0.79 (0.48, 1.30)	.01	.01	1.00 (0.98, 1.02)
Permissive parenting	–.07	.18	0.86 (0.53, 1.09)	–.10	.19	0.91 (0.63, 1.31)
Parental tolerance of risky behavior	.23*	.10	1.26 (1.04, 1.54)	–.11	.11	0.90 (0.72, 1.11)
Household rules	–.08	.05	0.93 (0.83, 1.04)	.03	.06	1.04 (0.92, 1.17)
Parent supervision	–.01	.14	0.99 (0.76, 1.30)	–.16	.15	0.85 (0.64, 1.13)
Sibling negative influence	. 32**	.13	1.39 (1.08, 1.78)	–.05	.15	0.95 (0.71, 1.26)
Peer context						
Peer attachment	.00	.01	1.00 (0.97, 1.04)	.01	.02	1.02 (0.98, 1.05)
Peer positive influence	.13	.08	1.14 (0.96, 1.36)	.25**	.09	1.28 (1.08, 1.53)
Peer negative influence	.10***	.02	1.11 (1.06, 1.16)	–.02	.02	1.03 (0.98, 1.07)
Unstructured social time	.72**	.26	2.07 (1.24, 3.44)	.06	.25	1.06 (0.65, 1.72)
School context						
Grades	–.17*	.10	0.84 (0.69, 1.00)	.25*	.12	1.29 (1.09, 1.69)
Organized activities	–.07	.11	0.93 (0.76, 1.15)	.36***	.11	1.44 (1.17, 1.78)
School changes	.02	.10	0.98 (0.81, 1.18)	–.15*	.10	0.86 (0.69, 1.00)
Community context						
Positive community resources	–.30*	.13	0.74 (0.57, 0.97)	.18*	.02	1.19 (1.03, 1.48)
Community control	–.05*	.02	0.93 (0.90, 0.99)	.00	.03	1.01 (0.94, 1.06)
Model fit						
–2 Log L	220.22		223.17			
Wald χ^2 ($df = 21$)	68.82***		41.87**			
Cox and Snell (1989) generalized R^2	.42		.21			

Note: All variables were entered simultaneously.
[a]1 = female, 0 = male. [b]1 = non-Hispanic White, 0 = all others. [c]1 = two-parent household, 0 = one-parent or other household. [d]1 = urban residence, 0 = rural residence.
*$p < .05$. **$p < .01$. ***$p < .001$.

less likely than boys to engage in health-promoting behavior over time.

How do interpersonal contexts affect adolescent behavior? To begin with, note that aspects of each of the interpersonal contextual domains were significantly associated with both sustained risky behavior and sustained health-promoting behavior. In terms of family relations, several aspects of parenting were associated with both negative and positive behavioral outcomes. First, authoritarian parenting was associated with a decreased likelihood of sustained risky behavior. In addition, parents' tolerance of risky behavior was associated with increased odds of sustained risky behavior. Moreover, with respect to positive behavior, parental attachment predicted increased odds of sustained health-promoting behavior. Beyond parental influences, the degree to which siblings engaged in risky behavior was also associated with an increased likelihood of engaging in risky behavior over time.

Several dimensions of the peer context had a significant influence on adolescent behavior. Peer negative influence and unstructured social time were both predictive of an increased likelihood of sustained risky behavior. On the other hand, adolescents who reported greater peer positive influence had increased odds of sustained health-promoting behavior over time. Attachment to peers, however, was unrelated to either risky or health-promoting behavior

With respect to the school context, the logistic regressions showed that adolescents who reported a greater connection to school, as proxied by grades, were less likely to engage in sustained risky behavior and more likely to engage in sustained health-promoting behavior than adolescents who did not. Adolescents' participation in organized activities after school was associated with increased odds of sustained health-promoting behavior. In addition, school (un)connectedness, marked by an increasing number of school changes, was associated significantly with lowered odds of sustained high health-promoting behavior.

Finally, two aspects of the community environment were associated with adolescents' behavior over time. Positive community resources for youth were associated with both a decreased likelihood of sustained risky behavior and an increased likelihood of sustained health-promoting behavior. Community control was associated with a decreased likelihood of sustained risk behavior over time.

Health Care Outcomes

The last analysis was to examine health care patterns for these adolescents over the 12-month period between Time 1 and Time 2. Adolescents who engaged in sustained risky behavior used more health care per month ($M = .59$, $SD = .87$) than those who did not ($M = .48$, $SD = .55$), $t(236) = 1.45$, $p < .07$. These adolescents also had higher expenditures ($M = \$131.71$, $SD = \$272.80$) than those who did not ($M = \$108.61$, $SD = \$243.93$), $t(237) = 1.36$, $p < .09$. In addition, on the health-promoting side, youth who engaged in sustained health-promoting behavior had fewer encounters with the healthcare system ($M = .42$, $SD = .44$) than those who did not ($M = .55$, $SD = .73$), $t(236) = 1.74$, $p < .05$. These adolescents were also less costly than their counterparts ($M = \$73.77$, $SD = \$151.28$ and $M = \$128.52$, $SD = \$274.68$, respectively), $t(237) = 1.78$, $p < .05$.

Discussion

The purpose of this study was to examine the relations between various aspects of multiple interpersonal contexts and adolescents' risky and health-promoting behavior and to examine health-care utilization outcomes for adolescents engaged in sustained risky or health-promoting behavior compared to those who were not. This study builds on previous research by simultaneously considering multiple key interpersonal domains, including both risk and protective factors, and by considering both risky and health promoting behavior. Several themes emerged from the analyses to highlight predictive relations between activities and resources for youth, interpersonal connections, control, and both risky and health-promoting behavior. Moreover, our analyses of health-care utilization based on engagement in risky and health-promoting behavior suggest health-care system targets for intervention, prevention, and the promotion of positive youth development. These issues are discussed in turn.

Activities and Resources for Youth

With respect to activities and resources for youth, we found that "hanging out" with peers in unstructured situations was associated with increased odds of risky behavior. Our findings also revealed that participation in school-related organized activities was health affirming. In other words, adolescents who participated in activities like sports and other organized extracurricular activities were more likely to engage in sustained health-promoting behavior. Moreover, beyond actual involvement, merely the knowledge that resources were available in the community had health-affirming benefits: adolescents' perceptions of the *availability* of positive community resources increased their odds of engaging in health-promoting behavior. Together, then, these findings are congruent with previous research about the importance of investing in resources and activities for youth in both reducing negative behavior but also promoting positive youth development (Mrazek et al., 2004; Roth & Brooks-Gunn, 2000; Taylor & Wang, 2000)

Interpersonal Connections

We also found evidence across relationship contexts about the importance influences of interpersonal "connections"—in both positive and negative ways. For example, in line with research that demonstrates positive connections between characteristics of families such as warmth and child outcomes (see, e.g., Cummings et al., 2000), adolescents in our study who reported warm, trusting relationships with their parents were more likely to engage in health-promoting behavior. These findings extended beyond the family as well, as our study also showed that positive peer influence was associated with sustained health-promoting behavior.

Our analyses also showed that negative interpersonal connections, characterized by negative influence and tolerance for risky behavior in the family and by peers were predictive of an increased likelihood of sustained risky behavior. Other research has highlighted the role of expectations about risky behavior in predicting problem behavior. Olds, Thombs, and Tomasek (2005), for example, found that intentions to initiate substance use were greater when youth believed their close peers and siblings were accepting of and more likely to use substances themselves. Moreover, adolescents who changed schools often, and were perhaps thereby deprived of opportunities to form bonds in the context of the school context, not only manifested a higher likelihood of risky behavior, but also decreased odds of engaging in health-promoting behavior.

Monitoring and Control

Several aspects of control were related to adolescent behavior. For example, congruent with other research (see Mrazek et al., 2004), our findings illustrate that adolescents' perceptions of community control may serve as a deterrent to risk behavior, as evidenced by its negative relationship to sustained risky behavior. Related to the parent–adolescent relationship, our findings showed that authoritarian parenting was associated in a protective way with decreased odds of risky behavior. Although it is generally argued that authoritarian parenting is not an optimal disciplinary strategy (Baumrind, 1989), given the nature of the sample, that is, a low-SES, high risk group, in this context, authoritarian parenting may have an adaptive protective influence. This argument is bolstered further by two bivariate correlations which, although not significant when all variables were entered in the full model, showed that parents who had clearer household rules and who engaged in greater supervision and monitoring of their youth had adolescents who were less likely to engage in risky behavior. Others stress the importance of parenting, monitoring, and supervision relative to problem behavior (Dishion & McMahon, 1998; Griffin et al., 2000; Rai et al., 2003).

Thus, with respect to the first goal of this study—to investigate the effects of risk and protective factors in multiple interpersonal contexts on sustained risky and health-promoting behavior—our findings add support to the growing literature stressing the importance of activities and resources for youth, interpersonal connections, and monitoring and control, in reducing risky and problem behavior. Our study also highlights the importance of considering these themes in relation to health promotion. Of note, different characteristics of each contextual setting were related to either risky or health-promoting behavior, implying potentially different targets for intervention related to either reducing negative behavior or increasing positive behavior. Together, however, these findings suggest that the most productive efforts to both ameliorate problem behavior, as well as promote health and competent behavior need to include multiple salient contexts—those close to the adolescent in their family and peer relationships, but also more broadly in mobilizing communities to support youth.

Policy Perspective

The second goal of our study was to examine health-care outcomes of adolescent positive and negative health-related behavior. These analyses showed increased health-care utilization and costs related to sustained risky behavior and decreased utilization and costs related to sustained health-promoting behavior. These findings point to an obvious window for risky behavior intervention and prevention, as well as positive health promotion—through the health care system. From a systems perspective, although there is general agreement among public health researchers that there are important developmental antecedents of risky and health-promoting behavior, there is a philosophical debate about whether or not it is the responsibility of the public health system to concern itself with identification, treatment and policies about those antecedents (Youngblade et al., 2006). One could argue that it is unfair to expect the health-care industry to finance treatment for outcomes owing to the contexts of adolescents' lives, but in fact, if one considers risky behavior a symptom rather than a unique causal event, the health care system already does. Analyses that specify which domains contribute differentially more to the prediction of risky behavior, and its costs, will be beneficial in terms of specifying education, prevention, and intervention programs that can be delivered through the health care system and via its links to social services. Thus, identifying contexts for prevention and health promotion may not only portend positive developmental outcomes for youth, but also positive effects for the health care system.

Limitations

This study had several limitations that should be highlighted. First, our study included a relatively small sample given the number of predictors. This is complicated by bias resulting from sample attrition. Although there were no significant differences in terms of risky or health-promoting variables, adolescents who remained in the longitudinal sample were somewhat younger and more likely to be girls than those who participated at the first time point only.

Second, this study utilized a more limited measure of health-promoting behavior as compared to our assessment of risk behavior. In part, this reflects the state of the literature, both conceptually and technically. That is, there is general consensus about classes of behaviors that are considered risky (e.g., substance use, injuries, unprotected sexual behavior), and there are numerous measurement batteries in the literature to assess single or multiple types of risky behavior. However, there is much less common ground in defining health-promoting behavior (Schulenberg et al., 1997). In some cases, health-promoting behavior refers to the absence of risky behavior whereas in other studies specific behaviors are identified (e.g., exercise, wearing seatbelts, etc.). In addition, distinctions are drawn between physical health-promoting behavior, and emotional health-promoting behavior (Heubner, 2003). Owing to these issues, measures of "health promoting behavior," including ours, are currently not well defined.

In addition, we examined multiple relationship *contexts*, but not all of our measures were measures of relationships. This was especially true for the school and community domains. Moreover, due to the length of our telephone survey, we did not assess all relationship contexts equally; for example, we had only one measure of the sibling relationship. Thus, while there are clear advantages of this study related to its breadth (i.e., a diverse, statewide sample who responded to a wide battery of measures of multiple contexts), there are limits related to depth.

Moreover, our measures all were obtained via self report from the target individual. Although perceptions are indeed salient for predicting behavior, a comprehensive understanding of the effects of "context" requires the inclusion of objective characteristics of environments as well (see Youngblade et al., 2006). Finally, this was a study of main effects. However, as with most contextual analyses, interactions between person and context, as well as interactions between relationship contexts, are potentially the most illuminating (e.g., Bronfenbrenner & Morris, 2006). Work we currently have in progress will address these issues.

Conclusion

Despite these limitations, our results suggest that both positive and negative health-related behavior have roots in multiple interpersonal contexts. In general, our findings showed that youth who were involved in contexts that provided positive resources and activities, who reported positive connections to multiple important others (i.e., parents, peers, community), and who were adequately monitored and controlled not only were less likely to engage in sustained high levels of risky behavior, but also were more likely to actively engage in health-promoting behavior. In addition, our results demonstrating health-care system outcomes related to both negative and positive health-related behavior add to policy discussions about targets for intervention, prevention, and the promotion of positive youth development.

References

Armsden, G., & Greenberg, M. T. (1987). The Inventory of Parent and Peer Attachment: Relationships to well-being in adolescence. *Journal of Youth and Adolescence, 18,* 683–692.

Bandura, A. (1977). *Social learning theory.* Englewood Cliffs, NJ: Prentice Hall.

Baumrind, D. (1989). Rearing competent children. In W. Damon (Ed.), *Child development today and tomorrow* (pp. 349–378). San Francisco: Jossey-Bass.

Benson, P. L., Leffert, N., Scales, P. C., & Blyth, D. A. (1998). Beyond the "village" rhetoric: Creating healthy communities for children and adolescents. *Applied Developmental Science, 2,* 138–159.

Biglan, A., Ary, D., Koehn, V., Levings, D., Smith, S., Wright, Z., et al. (1996). Mobilizing positive reinforcement in communities to reduce youth access to tobacco. *American Journal of Community Psychology, 24,* 625–638.

Bowlby, J. (1982) *Attachment and loss* (Vol. 1. Attachment, 2nd ed.). New York: Basic Books.

Bronfenbrenner, U., & Morris, P. A. (2006). The bioecological model of human development. In R. M. Lerner (Ed.), *Theoretical models of human development. Handbook of Child Psychology* (Vol. 1, 6th ed., pp. 793–828). New York: Wiley.

Catalano, R. F., & Hawkins, J. D. (1996). The social development model: A theory of antisocial behavior. In J. D. Hawkins (Ed.), *Delinquency and crime: Current theories* (pp. 149–197). New York: Cambridge University Press.

Cicchetti, D., & Aber, J. L. (1998). Contextualism and developmental psychopathology. *Development and Psychopathology, 10,* 137–141.

Coley, R. L., & Chase-Lansdale, P. L. (2000). Welfare receipt, financial strain, and African-American adolescent functioning. *Social Service Review, 74,* 378–405.

Cox, D. R., & Snell, E. J. (1989). *The analysis of binary data* (2nd ed.). London: Chapman & Hall.

Cummings, E. M., Davies, P. T., & Campbell, S. B. (2000). *Developmental psychopathology and family process.* New York: Guilford.

Curry, L. A., & Youngblade, L. M. (in press). Negative affect, risk perception, and adolescent risk behavior. *Applied Developmental Psychology.*

Developmental Research and Programs, Inc. (1999). *Communities that care youth survey.* Seattle, WA: Developmental Research and Programs, Inc.

Dishion, T. J., Capaldi, D., Spracklen, K. M., & Li, F. (1995). Peer ecology of male adolescent drug use. *Development and Psychopathology, 7,* 803–824.

Dishion, T. J., McCord, J., & Poulin, F. (1999). When interventions harm: Peer groups and problem behavior. *American Psychologist, 54,* 755–764.

Dishion, T. J., & McMahon, R. J. (1998). Parental monitoring and the prevention of child and adolescent problem behavior: A conceptual and empirical formulation. *Clinical Child and Family Psychology Review, 1,* 61–75.

Dryfoos, J. G. (1990). *Adolescents at risk: Prevalence and prevention.* New York: Oxford University Press.

East, P. L., & Jacobson, L. J. (2000). The younger siblings of teenage mothers: A follow-up of their pregnancy risk. *Developmental Psychology, 37, 254–264.*

Edelman, L. F., Bresnen, M., Newell, S., Scarbrough, H., & Swan, J. (2004). The benefits and pitfalls of social capital: Empirical evidence from two organizations in the United Kingdom. *British Journal of Management, 15,* S59–S69.

Elder, G. H., & Conger, R. D. (2000). *Children of the land: Adversity and success in rural America.* Chicago: University of Chicago Press.

Ferrer-Wreder, L., Stattin, H., Lorente, C. C., Tubman, J. G., & Adamson, L. (2004). *Successful prevention and youth development programs: Across borders.* New York: Kluwer Academic/Plenum.

Gardner, M., & Steinberg, L. (2005). Peer influence on risk taking, risk preference, and risky decision making in adolescence and adulthood: An experimental study. *Developmental Psychology, 41,* 625–635.

Gorman-Smith, D., Tolan, P. H., & Henry, D. (1999). The relation of community and family to risk among urban-poor adolescents. In P. Cohen, C. Slomkowski, & L. N. Robins (Eds.), *Historical geographical influence on psychopathology* (pp. 349–367). Mahwah, NJ: Lawrence Erlbaum Associates, Inc.

Griffin, K. W., Botvin, G. J., Scheier, L. M., Diaz, T., & Miller, N. L. (2000). Parenting practices as predictors of substance use, delinquency, and aggression among urban minority youth: Moderating effects of family structure and gender. *Psychology of Addictive Behaviors, 14,* 174–184.

Grunbaum, J. A., Kann, L., Kinchen, S. A., Williams, B., Ross, J. G., Lowry, R., et al. (2002). Youth risk behavior surveillance—United States, 2001. *Journal of School Health, 72,* 313–328.

Hawkins, J. D., Catalano, R. F., & Miller, J. Y. (1992). Risk and protective factors for alcohol and other drug problems in adolescence and early adulthood: Implications for substance abuse prevention. *Psychological Review, 112,* 64–105.

Heubner, A. (2003). Positive youth development: The role of competence. In F. A. Villarruel, D. F. Perkins, L. M. Borden, & J. G. Keith (Eds.), *Community youth development: Programs, policies, and practices* (pp. 341–357). Thousand Oaks, CA: Sage.

Hinde, R. A., & Stevenson-Hinde, J. (1987). Interpersonal relationships and child development. *Developmental Review, 7,* 1–21.

Hirschi, T. (1969). *Causes of delinquency.* Berkeley: University of California Press.

Irwin, C. E., Jr., Cataldo, M. F., Matheny, A. P., Jr., & Peterson, L. (1992). Health consequences of behaviors: Injury as a model. *Pediatrics, 90,* 798–807.

Jessor, R. (Ed.). (1998). *New perspectives on adolescent risk behavior.* New York: Cambridge University Press.

Jessor, R., Turbin, M., & Costa, F. (1998). Protective factors in adolescent health behavior. *Journal of Personality and Social Psychology, 75,* 788–800.

Johnston, L. D., O'Malley, P. M., & Bachman, J. G. (2001). *Monitoring the future: National survey results on drug use, 1975–2000. Vol. 1: Secondary school students.* Bethesda, MD: National Institute on Drug Abuse.

Klein, J. (1997). The National Longitudinal Study of Adolescent Health. Preliminary results: Great expectations. *Journal of the American Medical Association, 278,* 864–865.

Lerner, R. M., Lerner, J. V., Almerigi, J., Theokas, C., Phelps, E., Gestsdottir, S., et al. (2005). Positive youth development, participation in community youth development programs, and community contributions of fifth grade adolescents: Findings from the first wave of the 4-H Study of Positive Youth Development. *Journal of Early Adolescence, 25,* 17–71.

Lerner, R. M., & Simi, N. L. (2000). A holistic, integrated model of risk and protection in adolescence: A developmental contextual perspective about research, programs, and policies. In L. Bergman & R. Cairns (Eds.), *Developmental science and the holistic approach* (pp. 421–443). Mahwah, NJ: Lawrence Erlbaum Associates, Inc.

Maggs, J. L., Schulenberg, J., & Hurrelmann, K. (1997). Developmental transitions during adolescence: Health promotion interventions. In J. Schulenberg, J. L. Maggs, & K. Hurrelmann (Eds.), *Health risks and developmental transitions during adolescence* (pp. 522–546). New York: Cambridge University Press.

Moffitt, T. E, Caspi, A., & Rutter, M. (2001). *Sex differences in antisocial behavior: Conduct disorder, delinquency, and violence in the Dunedin Longitudinal Study.* New York: Cambridge University Press.

Morrill, R., Cromartie, J., & Hart, G. (1999). Metropolitan, urban, and rural commuting areas: Toward a better depiction of the United States settlement system. *Urban Geography, 20,* 727–748.

Mrazek, P. J., Biglan, A., & Hawkins, J. D. (2004). *Community-monitoring systems: Tracking and improving the well-being of America's children and adolescents.* Falls Church, VA: Society for Prevention Research.

Olds, R. S., Thombs, D. L., & Tomasek, J. R. (2005). Relations between normative beliefs and initiation intentions toward cigarette, alcohol, and marijuana. *Journal of Adolescent Health, 37,* 75.e7–75.e13.

Petraitis, J., Flay, B. R., & Miller, T. Q. (1995). Reviewing theories of adolescent substance use: Organizing pieces in the puzzle. *Psychological Bulletin, 117,* 67–86.

Practice Management Information Corporation. (1998). *Physician fees.* Los Angeles: Davis.

Rai, A. A., Stanton, B., Wu, Y., Li, X., Galbraith, J., Cottrell, L., et al. (2003). Relative influences of perceived parental monitoring and perceived peer involvement on adolescent risk behaviors: An analysis of six cross-sectional data sets. *Journal of Adolescent Health, 33,* 108–118.

Resnick, M. D., Bearman, P. S., Blum, R. W., Bauman, K. E., Harris, K. M., & Jones J., et al. (1997). Protecting adolescents from harm: Findings form the National Longitudinal Study on Adolescent Health. *Journal of the American Medical Association, 278,* 823–831.

Roth, J., & Brooks-Gunn, J. (2000). What do adolescents need for healthy development? Implications for youth policy. *Social Policy Report, Society for Research in Child Development, XIV*(1), 3–19.

Schulenberg, J., Maggs, J. L., & Hurrelmann, K. (Eds.). (1997). *Health risks and developmental transitions during adolescence.* New York: Cambridge University Press.

Silbereisen, R. K. (1998). Lessons learned—Problems to be solved. In R. Jessor (Ed.), *New perspectives on adolescent risk behavior* (pp. 518–543). New York: Cambridge University Press.

Sroufe, L. A. (1997). Psychopathology as an outcome of development. *Development and Psychopathology, 9,* 251–268.

Steinberg, L. (1987). Single parents, stepparents, and the susceptibility of adolescents to antisocial peer pressure. *Child Development, 58,* 269–275.

Steinberg, L., & Avenevoli, S. (1998). Disengagement from school and problem behavior in adolescence: A developmental–contextual analysis of the influences of family and part-time work. In R. Jessor (Ed.), *New perspectives on adolescent risk behavior* (pp. 392–424). New York: Cambridge University Press.

Taylor, R. D., & Wang, M. C. (Eds.). (2000). *Resilience across contexts: Family, work, culture, and community.* Mahwah, NJ: Lawrence Erlbaum Associates, Inc.

Tsai, W., & Ghoshal, S. (1998). Social capital and value creation: The role of intrafirm networks. *Academy of Management Journal, 41,* 464–476.

Udry, J. R., & Bearman, P. S. (1998). New methods for new research on adolescent sexual behavior. In R. Jessor (Ed.), *New perspectives on adolescent risk behavior* (pp. 241–269). New York: Cambridge University Press.

Youngblade, L. M., Col, J., & Shenkman, E. A. (2002). Health care use and charges for adolescents enrolled in a Title XXI program. *Journal of Adolescent Health, 30,* 262–272.

Youngblade, L. M., Curry, L. A., Novak, M. A., Vogel, W. B., & Shenkman, E. A. (2006). The impact of community risks and resources on adolescent risky behavior and health care expenditures. *Journal of Adolescent Health, 38,* 486–494.

Received September 15, 2005
Final revision received October 18, 2005
Accepted October 19, 2005

Applied Developmental Science
2006, Vol. 10, No. 2, 107–113

Understanding the Multiple Contexts of Adolescent Risky Behavior and Positive Development: Advances and Future Directions

John E. Schulenberg
Institute for Social Research, Department of Psychology, and Center for Human Growth and Development, University of Michigan

Several years ago when I was in graduate school in the Human Development and Family Studies program at Penn State (a place that connects many of us involved in this special issue), someone had put a little sign on a vacuum cleaner, which was kept in the corner of a student common room, that stated "No development happening here." It was funny at first and then just became part of the scenery. Of course development did not happen in a vacuum—we heard this in all our seminars and came to accept it as fact. Since that time, the interdisciplinary field of developmental science emerged (with roots in human ecology, lifespan development, and life course studies), distinct from the more organismic-based developmental psychology in its insistence that development can only be understood in relation to the multiple and multilevel contexts within which individuals are embedded. However, a fair criticism of our science is that despite knowing that we should attend to the multiple contexts in our studies, and even knowing quite a bit about how to do it, the field has not done so consistently or always proficiently.

Thus, the intent of this special issue, to bring more specific focus to how we think about and study the multiple contexts of adolescent development, is laudable. Together, the articles provide important insights into how the multiple features of young people's primary contexts and broader communities can influence development in positive and negative ways. Another key and commendable feature of this special issue is the integration of problem-focused etiological and prevention research concerning risky behaviors during adolescence (see *Applied Developmental Science* special issue on "Prevention as Altering the Course of Development," Maggs & Schulenberg, 2001) with the asset-focused research on positive youth development and promotion (see *Applied Developmental Science* special issue on "Conditions for Optimal Development in Adolescence," Csikszentmihalyi & Schneider, 2001). Clearly, these two facets of the adolescent development literature are related and have much to say to one another but typically have not engaged one another (Lerner, 2001). By having a more direct link between these two literatures, as this special issue provides, we can gain new insights about how both risky and positive behavior develop and interrelate, enriching theoretical and applied efforts in understanding and promoting optimal adolescent development. A third key and notable feature of this group of studies is the inclusion of a rich variety of samples of adolescents, many representing understudied populations. These and many other strengths of the four studies are discussed in this commentary. Like all good research, the studies raise numerous questions and issues, which also are considered here. This commentary is organized into four main interrelated topics: (a) studying contexts, (b) studying risky and positive behaviors, (c) causal relations, and (d) multiwave longitudinal data with representative samples. For each topic, I focus on the contributions and unique advances offered by the four studies, questions and issues raised by the studies, and future directions.

The author expresses his gratitude for the helpful comments of the special issue coeditors, the assistance of Ginny Laetz and Tanya Hart, and support from grants from the National Institute on Drug Abuse (DA01411) and the Robert Wood Johnson Foundation (032769).

Correspondence should be sent to John Schulenberg, Survey Research Center, Institute for Social Research, University of Michigan, Ann Arbor, MI 48106–1248. E-mail: schulenb@umich.edu

Studying Contexts

Each study provides unique contributions to the conceptualization and study of adolescents' contexts. The Youngblade and Curry (this issue) article focuses on the perceived interpersonal contexts of adolescents—specifically family (including both parent–adolescent and sibling–adolescent) relationships, and peer–adolescent relationships—along with school-related variables and perceptions of community resources, opportunities, and norms. Building nicely on previous theoretical and applied work, they consider how the various contextual risk and protective factors relate to risky and health-promoting behaviors over time. The breadth of this study in terms of measurement coverage, which is impressive, allows for needed insights into which features of the multiple contexts relate to risky and health-promoting behaviors, which in turn relate to health care system outcomes (a unique aspect of this study, as discussed later).

In the article by Graber, Nichols, Lynne, Brooks-Gunn, and Botvin (this issue), the emphasis is on multiple contexts—including family (adolescents' perceived parental monitoring), friends (adolescent reports of proportion of friends involved in delinquent activities), and media (self-reports of engagement with violent media)—and how they contribute to competent and problem behaviors concurrently and over time. Although parental monitoring and friends' delinquency have often been considered within the problem behavior literature, they have received relatively little attention in terms of competence outcomes. The focus on engagement with violent media (including music, movies, video games) is novel and, as it turns out, important because of its relation to problem and competent behaviors.

In the East, Weisner, and Reyes (this issue) article, the emphasis is on a largely unexamined feature of the family context for many adolescents—an older teenage sister's child. Specifically, they investigate the child care experiences adolescents have with nieces or nephews living with them, and how these experiences relate to positive and negative outcomes concurrently and over time. An important aspect of these analyses, which are based on data from adolescent self-reports, is the consideration of how the extent of child care interacts with the quality of experiences (in terms of learning about parenting and child care and in terms of negative emotions and drain on time), and this emphasis provides important new information about the developmental costs and benefits, especially over time, of family obligations.

The Theokas and Lerner (this issue) article is unique in the focus on actual features of young people's contexts and how the actual context relates to concurrent positive and negative developmental characteristics. Building on previous theoretical and empirical work, these authors provide a systematic categorization of ecological assets across different contexts (in this case, family, schools, and neighborhoods) in terms of human resources, physical and institutional resources, collective activity, and accessibility. They draw on multiple sources for their data, including adolescent and parent surveys, school administrator surveys, and various government reporting agencies regarding school and neighborhood assets. This mapping of the actual ecology of adolescents is, it appears, a complex and difficult endeavor but clearly satisfying in providing a more realistic and ultimately manageable consideration of the actual context.

What and How to Measure

We see considerable diversity across the studies in terms of what elements from the context are sampled for measurement, and how the various elements are measured. This is both a strength and a limitation, reflecting to some extent the state of the literature on measuring the context. Simply, there are fewer accepted standards about the measurement of the context compared to the measurement of individual characteristics. Of course, not all features of adolescents' salient contexts are included here, and some salient contexts (e.g., part-time work) are not represented. What comes through in this group of studies, however, is innovation and extension of what is typically measured: Youngblade and Curry (this issue) highlight sibling influence, *positive* peer influence, and positive resources and opportunities in the community, all prominent features of adolescents' contexts that are usually neglected; we see in the Graber et al. (this issue) study a focus on violent media, which constitutes a salient feature of adolescents' contexts that we as a field have been generally missing; East et al. (this issue) bring attention to an older teenage sister's child living in the family context as a central feature for younger siblings, which has been almost entirely ignored in past research; and Theokas and Lerner (this issue) make an unprecedented attempt to more fully embrace the actual context, focusing on multiple aspects of multiple contexts by drawing on multiple sources of data. Although it is worth pondering whether we as a science are yet to the point where we can consider more standards about how and what to measure in adolescents' contexts, these studies make a very strong case for examining both ecological assets and risk factors in our studies.

How Ecological Assets and Risk Factors Interrelate in Their Impact

Understanding how risk and protective factors relate to each other and contribute separately and jointly to difficulties has been one of the more enduring pursuits in research concerning problem behaviors and developmental psychopathology. Each of the studies here considers, through some type of regression analysis, how elements within and across contexts contribute uniquely to the positive and negative outcomes of interest. This strategy is commonly used and can offer an understanding of which features of the context are most influential in predicting the outcomes (while downplaying overlapping influences). In addition, interactions among features within and across contexts can help address questions about whether, for example, certain protective factors come into play at certain levels of risk. So, as East et al. (this issue) show, quantity and quality of the child care experience interact such that the effect of hours of child care depended on whether the experience was perceived as being good. When working across multiple contexts, the question is one of how cross-context ecological assets and risk factors interrelate in their influence—that is, a matter of mesosystem connections (Bronfenbrenner & Morris, 1998). Theokas and Lerner (this issue) consider correlations among the common ecological assets across the different contexts, and it is particularly interesting that indices of human resources were positively correlated across the family, school, and neighborhood. However, in the four studies, interactions of elements across different contexts were not considered in their impact on the risky and positive behaviors; this, of course, reflects a general tendency in the literature to not consider interactions, or to consider them but not find significant effects.

Future research ought to attend more to how contextual assets and risk factors work together to set the stage for risky and positive behaviors in young people. Multiplicative interactions are but one way of considering this. A tradition within developmental psychopathology has been to sum the number of contextual risk factors (e.g., Sameroff, 2000), addressing questions about the cumulative aspect of risk factors (and at the same time circumventing problems of overlap of effects among predictors); the same strategy could be used with contextual assets (e.g., see Benson, Scales, Hamilton, & Sesma, 2006). Another alternative, not necessarily captured by multiplicative interaction effects, is that assets and risk factors operate in a compensatory fashion, such that having positive opportunities and experiences in one context (e.g., school) compensates for having negative experiences in another (e.g., home). Thus, it may not be so much which contexts provide positive opportunities and experiences, but more a matter of having at least one enriched context that provides opportunities for thriving (see, e.g., Schulenberg, Bryant, & O'Malley, 2004). Alternatively, perhaps *which* specific enriched contexts are available for young people with specific needs or talents is the more important question in terms of compensatory effects. In any event, an emphasis on interactions among ecological assets and risk factors within and across contexts in terms of adolescent development can provide a more optimistic perspective for possible interventions by highlighting the multiplicity of health promotive configurations.

Distinction Between Actual and Perceived Context

Of particular interest in this special issue is the distinction between the perceived and actual context. The focus on the perceived context, often via self-report from the targeted young person, has been the typical approach and is used by three of the studies here. This is a reasonable approach, because it is likely that how one perceives elements in the context is as important, if not more important, than what might be called the objective or actual context. However, if we are to better understand causal relations involving person–context interactions, there needs to be an emphasis on the objective or actual context. We could ponder whether the context exists without being perceived by the targeted individuals, and challenge whether indeed there are any objective or actual features of the social context; or we could forge ahead, assuming that there are some agreed-on identifiable positive and negative aspects of the context, and try to draw better connections between perceived and actual contexts in our studies. Fortunately, Theokas and Lerner (this issue) venture down the latter path (guided partly by past work and a strong theoretical framework) and thus make an important unique contribution to the literature on context effects. Drawing connections between actual and perceived context is essential for future research (as is critical attention to how best to measure the actual and perceived context as noted above). In addition, it is important to consider the distinction between features available in the context, and those that individual adolescents engage—this is where individual selection characteristics come into play and help us take a few more steps toward the understanding of person–context interactions.

Multilevel Contexts

We know that contexts are multilevel—the individual is embedded within several primary contexts, which in turn are embedded in larger-scale social, cultural, technological, political, and economic contexts. Both Theokas and Lerner (this issue) as well as Youngblade and Curry (this issue) focus on the multilevel context by bringing in the broader community, and considering how it interrelates with the primary contexts to influence young people. As we see in these studies, the more proximal contexts, specifically families, emerge as more predictive of both positive and negative outcomes, a common finding in the literature on risk behaviors (e.g., Hawkins, Catalano, & Miller, 1992). Of course, this does not mean that the more distal contexts are unimportant. The meaning and functions of behaviors within proximal contexts can be better understood in light of the affordances and customs at the more distal level. Furthermore, typical regression approaches may not fully or fairly characterize the more distal context influences. For future analyses, using multilevel modeling analyses is an important way to consider, for example, how individuals are embedded in families which are embedded in communities, and how this multilayer embeddedness relates to outcomes of interest. This can help with parsing the overlapping influences across levels of context and provide understanding, for example, about how community assets are utilized differently by adolescents as a function of their families.

Continuity and Discontinuity of the Context

Continuity and discontinuity of context is also a critical feature in our understanding of the multiple contexts of young people, and although not a feature considered much in the studies here, it is one that clearly deserves attention in future longitudinal research. There is an assumption—a reasonable one to be sure—that there is considerable continuity in individual characteristics over time. Often, however, we fail to focus on the corresponding continuity of the context and the person–context interactions, which certainly contributes to continuity of individual characteristics. Likewise, changes in context and person–context interactions (say as a function of a major life transition or planned intervention) no doubt contribute to changes in behaviors and functioning for at least some young people (Schulenberg, Maggs, & O'Malley, 2003). A focus on continuities and discontinuities in the contexts of young people would broaden our understanding of the mechanisms of context effects on development by showing that it is not just amounts of ecological assets or risk factors at one point in time, but also the continuity and discontinuity of such assets and risk factors over time.

Studying Risky and Positive Behaviors

Across the studies, we see extensive diversity in what is considered in terms of risky and positive behaviors, their level of consideration (composite versus single sentinel scores), how they are examined, and language used to describe them. This diversity has many advantages, of course, and reflects the current state of the literature. It is safe to say that risky behaviors and positive behaviors constitute two very large and sometimes overlapping tents. Among the many topics that could be considered here, three will be briefly mentioned.

The first concerns the domains of and boundaries around risky and positive behaviors. As a field, we are better at conceptualizing and examining risky behaviors than positive behaviors. This is partly due to empirical experience, with risky behaviors (e.g., substance use, delinquency, risky sex) and indices of distress (e.g., depressive affect) being more of a longstanding concern in the literature than health promoting behaviors and positive mental health; but it may also be because risky behaviors are easier to identify and define and more likely to cluster together than positive behaviors, a statement that should be challenged in future research. Traditionally, the expectation is that risky and positive behaviors are negatively related, but this is worth challenging too. Specific risky and positive behaviors were unrelated in the Youngblade and Curry (this issue) article and only weakly related in the Graber et al. (this issue) study, and much can be gained in future research by understanding the cases where risky and positive behaviors are *positively* related. A related point here is that it is not always so easy to draw distinctions between risky and positive behaviors, for we know that many risky behaviors can sometimes have constructive aspects, in addition to destructive aspects, especially during late adolescence (e.g., Schulenberg & Zarrett, 2006).

A second and related topic is the need to examine risky and positive behaviors together in relation to multiple predictors. Indeed, an important set of advances that comes from this group of studies is how *both* ecological assets and risk factors relate to *both* risky and positive behaviors, giving us a fuller more realistic matrix of "inputs" and "outputs." We see in the Theokas and Lerner (this issue) article that certain ecological assets were related to both positive and negative behaviors; in the Graber et al. (this issue) article that ecological assets appear more pervasive in their influence than risk factors on problem and competent behaviors; and in the Youngblade and Curry (this issue) article, contextual protective factors were more related to health promoting behaviors and contextual risk factors were related to risky behaviors. Of particular interest in this regard is the study by East et al. (this issue) where positive and negative outcomes were found to commingle, and where a potentially negative situation for one sibling (becoming a teenage mother) resulted in positive outcomes for the other sibling (staying in school and not getting pregnant).

A third topic involves trajectories of risky and positive behaviors, and more broadly, multiple risky and positive pathways through adolescence. We know that behaviors tend to build on themselves over time such that the direction of development can often be discerned over two or more waves of data. Two of the studies consider change in outcomes over two waves, and as is clear, a more nuanced and complex picture emerges from moving target outcomes: Graber et al. (this issue) consider two sets of two-wave comparison, following outcomes across 6th to 7th grade and 7th to 8th grade, and show some important differences in outcomes across the two analyses, and Youngblade and Curry (this issue) build trajectory groups as outcomes and show how the contextual features relate to different patterns of change (and stability) in risky and positive behaviors over time. Future research would do well to focus on outcomes in terms of trajectories across multiple waves with growth modeling analyses that can permit, for example, the consideration of how multiple behaviors "travel together" over time. Furthermore, following from the emphasis on person–context interactions, considerations of individual similarities and differences in intraindividual change are essential, requiring less emphasis on normative trends in developmental change and more emphasis on different trajectories of change (Schulenberg et al., 2003); this can be considered, for example, through growth mixture modeling analyses. More broadly, these considerations indicate the need to focus on multiple pathways from ecological assets and risk factors to positive and negative outcomes, suggesting that across individuals, specific ecological assets (or risk factors) can lead to a variety of risky and positive outcomes—reflecting multifinality—and likewise, a variety of ecological assets and risk factors can lead to the same set of positive (or risky) outcomes—reflecting equifinality (Cicchetti & Rogosch, 2002).

Causal Relations

Each study yields causal inferences, cautiously worded and in the context of acknowledging study limitations. Each study is theoretically informed and carefully conducted. And each uses a correlational, rather than experimental, design. As developmental scientists, we typically are not able to directly address causal connections because often it is unethical, infeasible, or scientifically undesirable to conduct true experiments. We cannot, for example, randomly assign young people to chaotic family contexts or to strong, positive mesosystem links. Similarly, it would be artificial to assign young people to certain sports or activities, because it is likely that the choices young people make in selecting their own activities is part of the health-promoting aspect of such activities. Thus, preexisting differences and selection effects are ubiquitous challenges to our understanding of causal relations. More generally, these are the well-known problems of third variables and of endogeneity, where unconsidered, often developmentally prior, characteristics are causal agents in the relationships we examine (rendering them, to some degree, spurious), and where exogenous characteristics (assumed causes) are actually also consequences of the endogenous characteristics (assumed effects), respectively (Rutter, Pickles, Murray, & Eaves, 2001). Thus, what we may think are cause–effect connections are instead the playing out of relations that were already set in motion or the ongoing interplay of the variables such that causal direction is sometimes flipped.

Although such problems must be constantly acknowledged, it is worth challenging—just a bit—warnings about the dire validity problems of our correlational studies. From a developmental science perspective that draws on person–context interactionism (Lerner, 2006; Sameroff, 2000), it is the ongoing interaction between individuals and contexts that contributes to the direction of development, so it is inaccurate to suggest that picking up midstream in such relations is simply charting processes that are playing out their inevitable course set by unmeasured third variables. Rather, we likely are grasping part of the explanatory net when we examine how features of the context contribute to adolescent behavior in short-term longitudinal studies. Furthermore, it is expected in dynamic interactions between contexts and individuals that predictors (e.g., proportion of peers engaged in substance use) and outcomes (e.g., one's own substance use) reciprocally influence one another over time and that what is viewed as a cause of *A* is also, with time, a consequence of *A*. Thus, the endogeneity problem for developmental scientists is often not so much a threat to validity as it is a challenge to more accurately represent ongoing reciprocal relations between changing contexts and developing individuals. To be clear, this is not to champion the exclusive use of correlational designs—there is no doubt that such designs can lead us to causal errors that are problematic for our theories and interventions; rather, it is to argue that the complexity and activeness of development is such that theoretically informed, carefully conducted correlational studies can provide needed insight into ongoing causal relations.

The four studies appropriately attend to many potential third variable problems by including controls (e.g., age, race or ethnicity, gender) in the analyses, and they include longitudinal data or multimodal data that can help rule out some of the validity threats of correlational studies. In terms of future directions, planned and natural experiments would provide stronger evidence about how features of the context influence young people (Rutter et al., 2001). Ecologically valid and carefully controlled intervention studies are an important avenue, and it would be of considerable theoretical and practical importance to consider how various contextual interventions are related to positive (as well as negative) developmental outcomes. Also, although not experiments per se (because random assignment is still not possible), capturing naturally occurring events like major life transitions can provide important windows into understanding how changes in context relate to changing person–context interactions and individual outcomes (Schulenberg & Zarrett, 2006).

Multiwave Longitudinal Data From Representative Samples

Three of the studies are longitudinal, and the fourth is the first wave of a comprehensive longitudinal study. As we see in each of the longitudinal studies, a more complex and realistic story about development can be gained by examining relationships over time than by simply relying on within-time examinations. Indeed, the significance of these studies, as a whole, rests considerably on the inclusion of longitudinal data.

One clear avenue into advances in our understanding of problematic and optimal adolescent development involves the use of theoretically informed and methodologically rigorous multiwave longitudinal data gathered from representative samples. Of course, longitudinal data are not the cure-all and indeed include substantial problems of their own in terms of differential attrition (as we see in some of the studies here) and measurement problems. But without longitudinal data, we cannot advance our understanding of continuity of behavior and context or of temporal (and sometimes causal) relations. Although two waves of data can give us some leverage on these matters, three or more waves can yield much more by allowing us to better chart behavioral trajectories and to understand changes in trajectories as a function of changes in context such as major life transitions or planned interventions. The use of large and representative or otherwise well-characterized samples of individuals, as we see in some of the studies here, can offer a perspective on similarities and differences across individuals that we do not otherwise have. Again, large samples are not the cure-all, and they too have difficulties of their own in terms of resources. Still, without large, representative samples over time, it is difficult to examine differential developmental trajectories and multiple pathways.

Thus, many of the questions and issues posed in this commentary can be effectively addressed with multiwave longitudinal data from representative samples. We can examine with greater ease and clarity, for example, how multiwave trajectories of behaviors relate to multiwave trajectories of contexts, and how multiple pathways follow ecological assets and risk factors, illustrating equifinality and multifinality (Schulenberg, Sameroff, & Cicchetti, 2004). However, in the reality of finite resources, an important limitation of large-scale survey research is often that depth of measurement is not possible, indicating the clear need to combine large-scale research with smaller, in-depth studies. Furthermore, depending on the research question, targeted samples may be necessary, such as we see in the East et al. (this issue) study regarding younger siblings of teenage mothers. This highlights the importance of collaborations among theoretically compatible studies that vary in the breadth and depth of samples of individuals, of measures, and of measurement waves—very much like what is done in this special issue.

Conclusions

Inspired in part by this special issue, there is good reason to think that as a science, we will continue to progress to the point where we know as much about the conceptualization and study of contexts as we do about individual characteristics, setting the stage for even better understanding of person–context interactions. This set of studies provides additional evidence about the importance of such contextual characteristics as parental monitoring and peer deviance, new insights into features of adolescents' multiple contexts typically not considered (e.g., caring for nieces or nephews, engaging in violent media), and new inroads into how to measure the actual context. In addition to these contributions, strengths of this special issue include, for example, the integration of problem-focused research concerning risky behaviors and asset-focused research on positive development, as well as the rich variety of samples of adolescents. Building on these contributions and strengths, a central future challenge for our science includes how best to study contexts in terms of measuring the context, considering how ecological assets and risk factors work interactively, making connections between perceived and actual context, effectively exploiting the multilevel features of contexts, and examining the continuity and discontinuity of the context over time. Furthermore, attention needs to be given to various ways to study risky and positive behaviors (especially over time) and to alternative ways to examine causal relations. It is clear that the field at large could benefit from additional theoretically informed, multiwave, longitudinal studies based on large representative samples, especially when combined with smaller-scale, in-depth studies allowing us to more fully cover breadth and depth in samples of individuals, contexts, measures, and time points.

As noted in the overview by Youngblade and Theokas (this issue), an essential component of each study is the emphasis on applied implications, with each being ultimately concerned with promoting positive development in young people. While exercising appropriate caution, it is noteworthy that parental monitoring comes through as contributing to more positive and less risky behaviors in both the Youngblade and Curry (this issue) and the Graber et al. (this issue) studies. Similarly, in the Theokas and Lerner (this issue) study, collective activity within the family (including spending time together over dinner) relates quite strongly to more positive and fewer negative adolescent outcomes. Although selection effects and endogeneity problems cannot be ruled out, these findings join the growing evidence about the likely salutary effects of strengthening parent–adolescent relations (e.g., Dishion & McMahon, 1998). The East et al. (this issue) study yields important new findings that can be used in teen pregnancy prevention policy and programs. Of particular note, we can see based on the Youngblade and Curry study that benefits from increasing healthy and decreasing risky behaviors may well include lower need for health care services utilization.

Developmental science explicitly encourages interdisciplinary efforts, focusing on systems within the individual and those in which individuals are embedded. As gains continue to be made in understanding genetic through cultural influences on development, these gains can be productively incorporated into a developmental science framework. Simply, such influences cannot be fully understood without embedding them within the multiple contexts of development.

References

Benson, P. L., Scales, P. C., Hamilton, S. F., & Sesma, A. (2006). Positive youth development: Theory, research, and applications. In R. M. Lerner (Vol. Ed.), *Theoretical models of human development* (pp. 894–941). New York: Wiley.

Bronfenbrenner, U., & Morris, P. A. (1998). The ecology of developmental process. In W. Damon (Series Ed.) & R. M. Lerner (Vol. Ed.), *Handbook of child psychology: Vol. 1. Theoretical models of human development* (5th ed., pp. 993–1028). New York: Wiley.

Cicchetti, D., & Rogosch, F. A. (2002). A developmental psychopathology perspective on adolescence. *Journal of Consulting and Clinical Psychology, 70,* 6–20.

Csikszentmihalyi, M., & Schneider, B. (2001). Conditions for optimal development in adolescence: An experiential approach [Editors' Introduction to Special Issue]. *Applied Developmental Science, 5,* 122–124.

Dishion, T. J., & McMahon, R. J. (1998). Parental monitoring and the prevention of child and adolescent problem behavior: A conceptual and empirical formulation. *Clinical Child and Family Psychology Review, 7,* 61–75.

Hawkins, J. D., Catalano, R. F., & Miller, J. Y. (1992). Risk and protective factors for alcohol and other drug problems in adolescence and early adulthood: Implications for substance use prevention. *Psychological Bulletin, 112,* 64–105.

Lerner, R. M. (2001). Promoting promotion in the development of prevention science. *Applied Developmental Science, 5,* 254–257.

Lerner, R. M. (2006). Developmental science, developmental systems, and contemporary theories of human development. In R. M. Lerner (Vol. Ed.), *Theoretical models of human development* (pp. 1–17). New York: Wiley.

Maggs, J. L., & Schulenberg, J. (2001). Editors' introduction: Prevention as altering the course of development and the complementary purposes of developmental and prevention sciences. *Applied Developmental Science, 5,* 196–200.

Rutter, M., Pickles, A., Murray, R., & Eaves, L. (2001). Testing hypotheses on specific environmental causal effects on behavior. *Psychological Bulletin, 127,* 291–324.

Sameroff, A. J. (2000). Developmental systems and psychopathology. *Development & Psychopathology, 12,* 297–312.

Schulenberg, J. E., Bryant, A. L., & O'Malley, P. M. (2004). Taking hold of some kind of life: How developmental tasks relate to trajectories of well-being during the transition to adulthood. *Development & Psychopathology, 16,* 1119–1140.

Schulenberg, J. E., Maggs, J. L., & O'Malley, P. M. (2003). How and why the understanding of developmental continuity and discontinuity is important: The sample case of long-term consequences of adolescent substance use. In J. T. Mortimer & M. J. Shanahan (Eds.), *Handbook of the life course* (pp. 413–436). New York: Plenum.

Schulenberg, J. E., Sameroff, A. J., & Cicchetti, D. (2004). Editorial: The transition to adulthood as a critical juncture in the course of psychopathology and mental health. *Development & Psychopathology, 16,* 799–806.

Schulenberg, J. E., & Zarrett, N. R. (2006). Mental health during emerging adulthood: Continuity and discontinuity in courses, causes, and functions. In J. J. Arnett & J. Tanner (Eds.), *Coming of age in the 21st century: The lives and contexts of emerging adults* (pp. 135–172). Washington DC: American Psychological Association.

Received October 17, 2005
Final revision received October 30, 2005
Accepted October 31, 2005

For Product Safety Concerns and Information please contact our EU representative GPSR@taylorandfrancis.com Taylor & Francis Verlag GmbH, Kaufingerstraße 24, 80331 München, Germany

T - #0207 - 270225 - C0 - 280/208/3 - PB - 9780805893816 - Gloss Lamination